Behind the Scenes of
They Were Expendable

Behind the Scenes of *They Were Expendable*

A Pictorial History

Lou Sabini
with Photographs by
Nicholas Scutti

Forewords by
Scott Eyman and Karen Everson

McFarland & Company, Inc., Publishers
Jefferson, North Carolina

Library of Congress Cataloguing-in-Publication Data

Sabini, Lou, 1952–
Behind the scenes of They were expendable : a pictorial history / Lou Sabini with photographs by Nicholas Scutti ; forewords by Scott Eyman and Karen Everson.
    p.   cm.
Includes bibliographical references and index.

ISBN 978-0-7864-9500-9 (softcover : acid free paper) ∞
ISBN 978-1-4766-1975-0 (ebook)

1. They were expendable (Motion picture)   I. Scutti, Nicholas, 1926–   II. Title.
PN1997.T4278S33 2015   791.43'72—dc23   2015016036

British Library cataloguing data are available

© 2015 Lou Sabini and Nick Scutti. All rights reserved

No part of this book may be reproduced or transmitted in any form or by any means, electronic or mechanical, including photocopying or recording, or by any information storage and retrieval system, without permission in writing from the publisher.

Front cover: Nick Scutti and Robert Montgomery on the set of *They Were Expendable* (from the collection of Nicholas Scutti).

Printed in the United States of America

*McFarland & Company, Inc., Publishers
Box 611, Jefferson, North Carolina 28640
www.mcfarlandpub.com*

*To Louis J. Sabini (1920–2008) and
William K. Everson (1929–1996);
My father shaped by character...
My friend and mentor shaped my career.*
—L.S.

*To Paul, Jim and Stephen, my sons;
My wife, Ann;
and my three grandchildren,
Christopher, Michaela and Dominic.*
—N.S.

TABLE OF CONTENTS

Acknowledgments by Lou Sabini	9
Foreword by Scott Eyman	11
Foreword by Karen Everson	13
Introduction	15
I: An Overview of the Film and Its Making	19
II: The Photographer	42
III: The Photographs	58
IV: The Real Heroes	153
V: The Celluloid Heroes and Supporting Cast	157
Appendix 1—Promotion, Reviews and Critical Reception	167
Appendix 2—Kelly v. Loew's, Inc.	171
Bibliography	193
Index	195

Acknowledgments

by Lou Sabini

There are so many individuals I must thank to express my deep appreciation for all they've done to make this book a reality. First and foremost, I wish to thank Nick Scutti. Without him, this documentation of a significant portion of the making of *They Were Expendable* would not exist. Nick's dedication to this project, making sure that all of the photographs were captioned and enhanced made the writing of this book a delight. I have never met a nicer man and I am proud to have worked with him. Another gentleman who deserves my sincerest thanks is Dan Burke who, while working at the Stamford Historical Society in Stamford, Connecticut, had emailed me a couple of photographs that Nick had taken while on the set of *They Were Expendable*. Naturally, they intrigued me and I asked Dan for Nick's telephone number, hoping to write an article on Nick's "day" on the set of this classic movie. Little did I realize that Nick had been on the set for the entire location shoot and took close to 150 pictures.

Special thanks must go to film scholar Scott Eyman, who has written a foreword for my book. Scott is the preeminent authority on the lives and careers of John Ford and John Wayne. I am extremely honored…

Another dear friend who was always there for me was Karen Latham Everson, a woman for whom I have the deepest respect. She has always given me the best suggestions and, being a huge John Ford fan, was very helpful when I would occasionally experience writer's block with my project. I also wish to thank Melanie Wyler, who suggested that I attend a book signing at the Westport Library in Westport, Connecticut, to meet Bill Levy,

Acknowledgments by Lou Sabini

who had just written a book, *Lest We Forget*, on John Ford's stock company. Bill and I immediately hit it off and it was through Bill that I was able to contact many people who have aided me not only with the book, but with getting it published. Bill hooked me up with James Parish, Tag Gallagher, April Lane ("Directed by John Ford" website) and especially Dan Ford. Through Dan Ford, I was able to receive permission from Ethan Wayne (John Wayne Enterprises) to use the images of his father in my book. Speaking of images, special thanks must go to my good friend, John McElwee, for supplying me with stills from *They Were Expendable.* My very good friend, Andy Dzamba, was always there to make great suggestions and guide me whenever I began to lose track. Also, thanks must go to Nick Scutti's good friend, photographer Richard H. Robertson, who took extreme care in digitizing each of the pictures. The results were absolutely outstanding!

Other individuals I would like to thank are: Richard W. Bann, Richard Barrios, Ralph Celentano, Robert Cline, John Duff III, Rich Finegan, Eric Grayson, Rosemary Hanes (Library of Congress), Jeffry Heise, Ron Hutchinson (The Vitaphone Project), Bruce Lawton, Rick Lertzman, Annette D'Agostino Lloyd, Scott and Jan MacGillivray, Mark McDade, Gerry Orlando, Jenny Paxson (Library of Congress), Jack Roth, Carol Rugh, Lauren Sabini, Brent Seguine, Janice Balog Spahn, Stan Taffel, Frank Thompson, and Jordan Young for their suggestions and guidance. I would also like to thank the man who was my inspiration from that very first day I walked into my first film history class at Manhattan's School of Visual Arts, William K. Everson, who made my life so special through his kindness, generosity and knowledge. Our friendship lasted close to 25 years and looking back, I couldn't have found a better mentor.

Lastly, I want to thank the very special lady, who has been my "right-hand man," so to speak, my wife and partner of more than 40 years, Susan Sabini. This highly remarkable woman has watched every solitary motion picture I have seen in these past four decades and has kept a log of every single title (I think she's up to her twelfth volume).

Her suggestions, our discussions and her positive attitude have made my life so special and I couldn't imagine a day without her. Our lives together bring to mind a classic William Wyler title, *The Best Years of Our Lives.*

Foreword

by Scott Eyman

The adjudications of history are never final—was Richard III a misunderstood hero or a deep-dyed villain? It all depends on who you ask and the current state of the evidence. Even though the movies are only slightly more than a century old, nothing much is certain there either … except for the fact that John Ford remains the directorial gold standard, so much so that he's never even been successfully imitated, unless you count some of Ford's own efforts when the tank was trending toward "empty."

So Lou Sabini's discovery of a batch of heretofore unknown production photographs from *They Were Expendable* is extremely meaningful, not just because the sets appear to have been built not that far away from Collins Avenue on Miami Beach instead of the reported location of Key Biscayne— the probable shooting spot for the second unit commanded by James Havens. It's because the shots show Ford and company clear, without any staging from a studio-hired cameraman. John Wayne is relaxed and having a good time, just as his co-workers said was usually the case, and even the notably chilly Robert Montgomery seems to be enjoying himself.

As for Ford himself, he's obviously in total control—the cast and crew are often looking at him—but he's also slightly apart from everybody else, as well he might have been. *They Were Expendable* is one of the most paradigmatic works in the Ford canon, and also among the most subjective, depending on your level of maturity. When I first saw it, in my early 20s, it struck me as attractively moody but slightly dull. That whooshing sound I should have heard was the movie passing far over my head.

Foreword by Scott Eyman

When I saw it again 15 years later, my experience of life's compromises and inevitable failures had deepened, and I was able to see it clear. And when I look at it now, nearly 40 years after I first watched it, it seems to me an old man's movie far before its—or Ford's—time. Not a film about triumph, as might have been expected for a movie made as World War II was winding down, but a film about adults coping with failure and loss: the universal human experience.

Today, it seems to me one of Ford's greatest movies, right up there with *My Darling Clementine* and *The Searchers*—movies that you can look at for a lifetime and never get to the bottom of.

The evidence is right there on the screen—and in these remarkable photographs.

Scott Eyman is the author of *Print the Legend: The Life and Times of John Ford*, and *John Wayne: The Life and Legend*. He has written numerous other books about the Golden Age of Hollywood, and lectures around the world on the subject of film.

Foreword

by Karen Everson

I've loved movies all my life, and growing up I loved them more enthusiastically and knew more about them than anyone else in my circle of friends and family. It was only when I got to New York University and met my future husband, William K. Everson, that I realized how little I knew.

Bill was an ocean of information. He not only knew facts, but he also understood context. He could tell you why a film was made the way it was when it was, and what made it work so well. And his list of "best movies" or "favorite movies" wasn't like most other such lists you might find. He didn't include the usual titles like *Shane* or *Citizen Kane.* And although he loved John Ford's body of work and greatly admired his talent, Bill didn't put *Stagecoach* or *The Searchers* or *The Man Who Shot Liberty Valance* at the top of his list. His favorite Ford movies were *The Sun Shines Bright, Wagon Master* and *They Were Expendable.* He liked the first for its comedy and "the kind of sentiment that only Ford and Frank Borzage could pull off"; and the second because he saw it as a "quiet, simple, austere little western—the sort of western Bill Hart would have approved of."

As for the third, Bill saw *They Were Expendable* as a very personal (for Ford, the Navy man), very realistic, and not overly glamorized war film. In fact, as he said in program notes written for a 1973 screening, *They Were Expendable* "was an odd film indeed to make at the close of a war. Its sadness and melancholy hardly matched the jubilation of the period, it had little propagandist value, and yet it was still too soon for it to have real perspective on the late war.... Nevertheless it was not only one of the best of

Foreword by Karen Everson

the war films, but in many ways one of Ford's own best films." He liked the way the film depicted the "exhilaration that war can bring at those moments when unity, comradeship, a just cause and lucky breaks coincide" to make things go right. He praised its "superb photography and excellent 2nd-unit staging" and said that the torpedo-run sequences were staged "almost like seagoing equivalents of a Ford cavalry charge."

He was pleased that Robert Montgomery was cast in what would typically be considered the "John Wayne role" and felt that this showed "the measure of Ford's restraint." He liked what he called the "underplayed romance" between John Wayne and Donna Reed, and the serenading scene so much like the Sons of the Pioneers singing in *Rio Grande*. Bill loved seeing "grand old-timers" such as Jack Holt, and Robert Barratt, almost unrecognizable as General MacArthur; the usual members of Ford's stock company such as Jack Pennick, Ward Bond, and Russell Simpson; the use of "Red River Valley" in Simpson's scenes, and the fact Ford was able to make it work "without seeming mawkish or contrived."

Bill's sense of what made a movie great certainly shaped the way I watch movies today. I learned so much from him. So did Bill's friend and one-time student, Lou Sabini. Lou is *my* friend, too, and I can detect Bill's influence when I hear Lou's enthusiasm for this or that movie, this or that director or actor.

I know that Bill would be as excited as I am to see this book in print. He'd have loved to see Nick Scutti's amazing photographs. And he would be proud of his friend Lou for working so hard to make the project a reality.

It's really "swell"!

Karen Latham Everson has a master's degree in cinema studies from New York University. During her marriage to the film scholar William K. Everson, she attended multiple daily screenings and participated in discussions on all aspects of film history. She now lives in Texas and works as a licensed professional counselor.

INTRODUCTION

Writing about classic movies these days can be a rather difficult endeavor, considering the fact that most of the actors, directors and technicians involved in their making have all left us. All we can rely on now are old interviews, articles and stories told so long ago that they have now fallen into the realm of Hollywood folklore. Newer films have the distinct advantage through modern technology to not only provide audio commentary by the filmmakers and actors, but to also feature additional materials, such as filmed documentaries as well as "director's cuts" of the movies.

Sadly, during Hollywood's Golden Era, none of this was made accessible to the viewing public. Certainly, studios like MGM, Paramount, Warner Bros. and others would produce "candidly" filmed short subjects giving the viewer an inside peek into the making of some of the studios' bigger hits. All of these curiosities are fun and fascinating to watch today, although they are clearly over-rehearsed, with the actors seemingly ill at ease. As for out-takes, MGM always was adamant about not releasing footage of their stars missing their cues or flubbing their lines, while Warner Bros. would produce an annual short subject of outtakes for studio personnel consumption only. Interestingly, all of these one-reel delights exist today and have been included as extras on many of the Warner DVDs which have been produced over the last few years.

While many classic movies now available on DVD have many extras such as trailers, audio commentary and even new documentaries, much of this information is being translated by people who have done a great deal of research, but too often their conclusions can be challenged, and varying accounts of what occurred on which set become mere conjecture. In the

Introduction

1962 John Ford film, *The Man Who Shot Liberty Valance*, a famous quote went "When the legend becomes fact, print the legend." In many instances this has occurred, due to embellished accounts by the stars, directors or technicians.

Being able to chronicle the filming of a classic movie today seems to be an almost impossible task, especially when the director happens to be a Hitchcock, Capra, Sturges, Wyler, Wellman, Hawks or other filmmakers of that era. That is, unless you come across a golden opportunity like I did in June of 2012 when a good friend of mine, Dan Burke, who was working at the Stamford Historical Society in Stamford, Connecticut, contacted me. Being Stamford natives, both of us are naturally interested in the historical background of our city, and Dan occasionally forwarded me fascinating little tidbits about our hometown, the place where my father was born and where my grandparents settled after docking on Ellis Island in 1902.

On one particular occasion, Dan forwarded me three fascinating

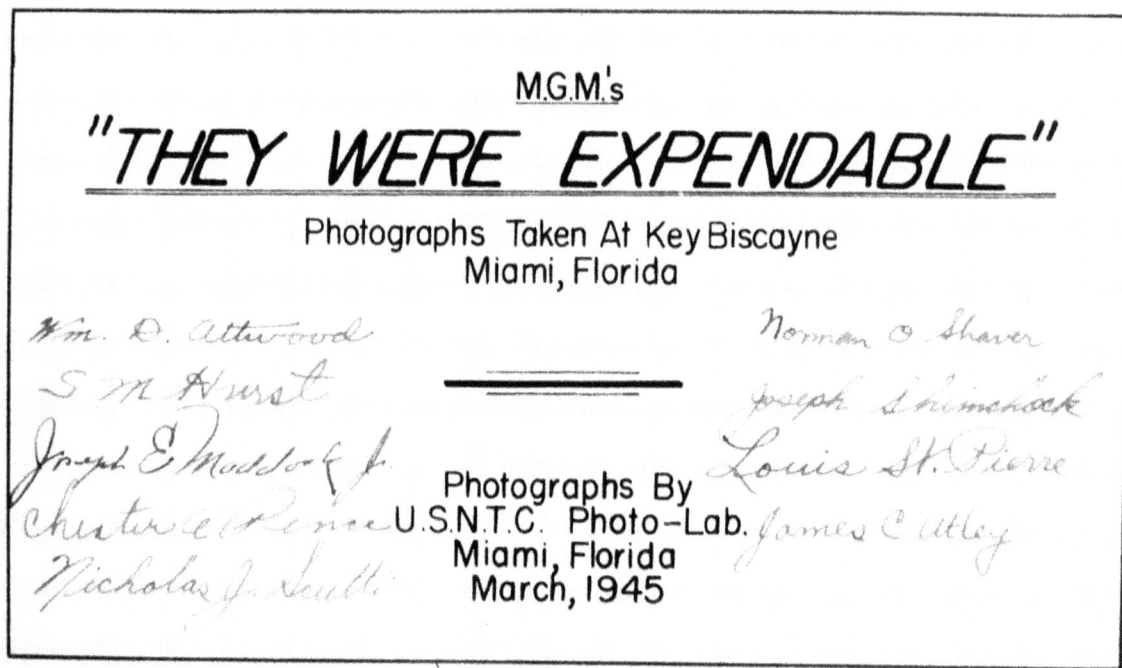

Names of all the Naval Lab photographers from the United States Naval Training Center. Not one foot of film was shot on Key Biscayne as MGM publicists implied.

Introduction

Members of the U.S. Training Center Photographic Lab. Top row (left to right): S. M. Hurst (photographer's mate 2nd class), Lieutenant Stevens, Joseph Maddock (photographer's mate 1st class). Second row: Donald L.A. White (photographer's mate 2nd class), Chester A. Pence (seaman 1st Class), James C. Utley (photographer's mate 3rd class). Bottom row: William D. Atwood (seaman 1st class), Nick Scutti (seaman 1st class), Louis St. Pierre (photographer's mate 2nd class), Norman O. Shaver (photographer's mate 3rd class).

Introduction

snapshots taken on location during the filming of the 1945 John Ford classic, *They Were Expendable*, one of which was a photograph of director John Ford casually lying on the ground and having a discussion with Robert Montgomery and John Wayne. Another showed Robert Montgomery sitting on a navy truck with a young unidentified sailor, who I later discovered was the person responsible for the photographs, a man named Nick Scutti. According to Dan, Nick was stationed in Miami, Florida, at the Sub Chaser Training Center, working as a naval photographer. I asked Dan if Nick would be interested in allowing me to interview him for a possible newspaper article.

When I telephoned Nick, he seemed genuinely enthusiastic and he invited me to come over. Bringing my wife Sue as my stenographer, I began asking Nick various questions about the time he spent on the shooting location. To my utter astonishment, he told me that he was there for the whole 30 days of location shooting, which was shot not on Key Biscayne—as all documents have reported—but filmed on a small uninhabited island off the coast of Miami. Adding to my delight was the fact that Nick had taken about 150 photographs chronicling the whole series of events during the location shooting. After flipping through the collection, I was convinced that a mere article wasn't enough and a whole book might be more appropriate. Luckily, he had the wherewithal to number each and every snapshot, which gives an account of each day's work on the set as well as which scenes were shot first and where.

My initial meeting with Nick Scutti was filled with fascinating anecdotes about Ford, Wayne, Montgomery and many of the people who worked on this classic wartime drama. His memory is truly unbelievable and I found him to be a most delightful man, who really loved being on the set daily, sitting in very close proximity to Mr. Ford. All of his recollections can be found in this comprehensive volume for all film students and fans to enjoy. I certainly hope that there might be someone someplace who had a similar experience to Nick's on a movie set. Perhaps they will come forth and share their experiences for all classic film lovers to embrace.

I: Overview of the Film and Its Making

They Were Expendable (1945) MGM. Produced and Directed by John Ford (Captain U.S.N.R.). Associate Producer: Cliff Reid. Based on the book by William L. White. Screenplay by Lieutenant Commander Frank Wead and Jan Lustig. Musical Score by Herbert Stothart. Art Direction by Cedric Gibbons and Malcolm Browne. Photography by Joseph H. August (Lt. Comdr. U.S.N.R.). Special Effects by A. Arnold Gillespie, Donald Jahraus, R.A. MacDonald. Edited by Frank E. Hull and Douglass Biggs. Set Decorations by Edwin B. Willis. Sound by Douglas Shearer. Costumes by Yvonne Wood. Make-up by Jack Dawn and Sam Palo. Unit Manager: Gilbert Kurland. Second Unit Director: James C. Havens U.S.M.C.R. Assistant Director: Edward O'Fearna and Jack Pennick. Associate Set Decorator: Ralph S. Hurst. Propman: Neil Wheeler. Re-Recording and Effects Mixers: James Z. Flaster, Robert Shirley, Newell Sparks, William Steinkamp, John A. Williams. Unit Mixer: Lowell Kinsall. Sound Effects by Michael Steinore. Visual Effects by Mark Davis, Donald Jahraus, Warren Newcombe. Stunts by Jack Stoney. Assistant Cameramen: Emilo Calori and Herbert Fischer. Additional Orchestrations by Harold Byrns, Murray Cutter, Wally Heglin, Alberto Colombo. Music Mixers: M.J. McLaughlin, Herbert Stahlberg. Stock Music Composed by Eric Zeisl. Script Clerk: John Banse. Assistant Research Director: Gladys Norvell. Research by George Richelavie. Technical Advisor: Ernest Seftig. Song: *To the End of the End of the World* by Earl Brent and Herbert Stothart. 135 min.

CAST: Robert Montgomery (Lieutenant John Brickley), John Wayne (Lieutenant [JG] "Rusty" Ryan), Lieutenant Sandy Davyss (Donna Reed), Jack Holt (General Martin), Ward Bond (Chief Petty Officer Boat-Wain Mate "Boats" Mulcahey), Marshall Thompson (Ensign Snake Gardner), Paul Lang-

Behind the Scenes of *They Were Expendable*

ton (Ensign "Andy" Andrews), Leon Ames (Major James Morton), Arthur Walsh (Seaman Jones), Donald Curtis (Lieutenant "Shorty" Long), Cameron Mitchell (Ensign George Cross), Jeff York (Ensign Tony Aiken), Murray Alper ("Slug" Mahan), Harry Tenbrook ("Squarehead" Larsen), Jack Pennick ("Doc"), Alex Havier (Benny Lecoco), Charles Trowbridge (Admiral Blackwell), Robert Barrat (General Douglas MacArthur), Bruce Kellogg (Elder Tompkins), Tim Murdock (Ensign Brown), Louis Jean Heydt (Ohio), Russell Simpson (Dad Knowland), Pedro deCordoba (The Priest), Vernon Steele (Army Doctor at Corregidor), Tom Tyler (Captain at Airport), Trina Lowe (Gardner's Girlfriend), Stubby Kruger, Sammy Stein, Blake Edwards, Michael Kirby (Boat Crew), Robert Emmett O'Connor (Bartender, Silver Dollar), Phillip Ahn (Army Orderly), Steve Barclay (Naval Officer), Bill Barnum, Art Foster, Del Hill, Michael Kirby, Ted Lundigan, Danny Borzage (Boat Crew Members), Alan Bridge (Lieutenant Colonel), George Bruggeman (Man in Admiral's Office), Pacita Tod-Tod (Filipino Girl Singer), William B. Davidson (Hotel Manager), Max Ong (Mayor of Cebu), Bill Wilkerson (Sergeant Smith), John Carlyle (Lieutenant James), Betty Blythe (Officer's Wife), Kermit Maynard (Officer at Airport), Charles Calhoun, James Carlisle, Gary Delmar, Frank Donahue, Leonard Fisher, Dick Karl (Men in Admiral's Office), John Carlyle (Lieutenant James), Jack Carrington (Officer at Airport), Bruce Carruthers, Tony Carson, Michael Kostrick, Paul Kruger, Jack Lee, Jack Lorenz, James Magill, George Magrill, Leonard Mellin, Karl Miller, Wedgwood Nowell, Dan Quigg, Clifford Rathjen, John Roy, Harold Schlickenmayer, Jack Semple, Sam Simone, Reginald Simpson, Lee Stanford, Larry Steers, Bob Thom, Roy Thomas, Richard Thorne, Brad Towne (Men in Admiral's Office), Jack Cheatham (Commander), Fred Coby, Roger Cole, William 'Red' Donahue, Frank Eldredge, John Epper, Charles Ferguson, Donald S. Lewis, Bill Nind (Officers at Airport), Jane Crowley (Officer's Wife), Henry H. Daniels, Jr. (Sailor), Marjorie Davis (Nurse), Patrick Davis (Pilot), Larry Dods, Frank Pershing, Robert Shelby Randall, Joey Ray, William McKeever Riley, Phil Schumacher, Jack Stoney (Boat Crew Members), Ernest Dominguez (Filipino Boy), George Economides, Michael Economides (Bartender's Children), Jim Farley, Wallace Ford (Bits), Lee Tung Foo (Asian Bartender), Almeda Fowler (Officer's Wife), Mary Jane French (Lost Nurse), Jon Gilbreath (Submarine Commander), Duke Green (PT-41 Boat Starboard Torpedoman), Sherry Hall (Marine Major), Robert Emmett Homans (Bartender at Manila Hotel), Vincent Isla (Filipino Schoolteacher), Leota Lorraine (Officer's Wife), Jack Luden

Opposite: **Original edition of the book *They Were Expendable* by W. L. White.**

THEY WERE EXPENDABLE

W. L. WHITE

(Naval Air Captain), Eve March (Nurse), Kermit Maynard (Airport Officer), Merrill McCormick (Wounded Officer at Airport), Frank McGrath ("Slim"-Bearded CPO), Henry Mirelez (Filipino Boy), Margaret Morton (Bartender's Wife), Jack Mower (Officer), Charles Murray, Jr. (Jeep Driver), Forbes Murray (Navy Captain), Bill Neff (Submarine Skipper), Franklin Parker (Naval Officer), Nino Pipitone, Jr. (Bartender's Child), Jack Ross, Brent Shugar, Robert Strong, Jack Trent, Hansel Warner (Officers at Airport), Ernest Seftig (Naval Officer), Leslie Sketchley (Marine Orderly), Ralph Soncuya (Filipino Orderly), Emmet Vogan (Naval Doctor), Eleanor Vogel (Officer's Wife), Billy Wilkerson (Sergeant Smith), Roque Ybarra, Jr. (Bartender's Child).

John Ford

American film pioneer John Ford is usually associated with classic westerns, which he began making in the silent era with veteran cowboy star, Harry Carey, Sr. Throughout his nearly 60 years as a director, he turned out more classics in that particular genre than any other director past or present. Films like *Straight Shooting* (1917), *The Iron Horse* (1924), *Three Bad Men* (1926), *Stagecoach* (1939), *My Darling Clementine* (1946), *Three Godfathers* (1949), *Wagon Master* (1950), *The Searchers* (1956) *The Man Who Shot Liberty Valance* (1962), not to mention his cavalry trilogy, *Fort Apache* (1948), *She Wore a Yellow Ribbon* (1949) and *Rio Grande* (1950) are all studied and revered by critics and film students even to this day.

Although his love for the Old West is evident in many of his films, I've always found it rather curious that his first western "talkie" came as late as 1939 with the release of *Stagecoach*, which put John Wayne's name on the map as a major leading man, after having worked in silents as a mere extra and in low budget "B Oaters" as they were referred to.

Ford didn't make any westerns during this period due to the fact that by the early thirties, westerns (like musicals) had gone out of fashion with the public, and were now considered passé. As a result, only low budget "B" westerns were being produced in abundance, which were aimed primarily for youngsters. There were some exceptions throughout the decade, however (e.g., *Cimarron* and *The Plainsman*), but these ventures were few and far between. Then, in January of 1939, Twentieth Century–Fox released a big-budget Technicolor western, *Jesse James*, starring Tyrone Power and Henry Fonda, which brought in large revenues at the box office as well as excellent reviews.

I. Overview of the Film and Its Making

Coincidentally, around the same time that *Jesse James* was in production, John Ford wanted to make a western, based on the short story by Ernest Haycox called *Stage to Lordsburg*. Produced independently by Walter Wanger and released through United Artists, *Stagecoach* is still considered one of the greatest westerns ever made, even though there was a lot of turbulence "behind the scenes" between Wanger and Ford.

Initially, Ford had approached John Wayne, whose career had really taken a nosedive after being cast in the big-budget western *The Big Trail* in 1930, which was directed by Raoul Walsh. Filmed in experimental widescreen 65mm, the film proved to be a tremendous flop at the box office and Wayne was relegated to making low budget westerns thereafter. When Wayne read the script to *Stagecoach*, Ford asked him who would be a good choice to play the Ringo Kid. Wayne pondered for a moment (hoping that Ford might select him) and blurted Lloyd Nolan. After much discussion, Ford finally told Wayne that he would like him to play the part, which Ford knew would be a "star-making" role for the 31-year-old actor.

This would have been Wayne's 80th picture, but when producer Wanger heard that Ford had cast Wayne, he kept reminding the persistent director about *The Big Trail* fiasco and insisted on getting Gary Cooper. Ford would have none of it (but did screen test Bruce Cabot to appease Wanger) and stayed adamant with casting Wayne.

Critically and financially, *Stagecoach* was a resounding smash hit and Wayne was on the way to becoming a superstar. As a result, other major westerns were released in quick succession in 1939, including, *Dodge City, The Oklahoma Kid, Union Pacific, Destry Rides Again* and many others. Once World War II broke out, however, westerns were again phased out for a spell in favor of war films. Fortunately, by 1946, the American western was experiencing another resurgence which lasted throughout the sixties.

Ford's non-western films are equally as good, especially when the director had a particular interest in the project, such as *The Informer* (1935), *The Grapes of Wrath* (1940) and *How Green Was My Valley* (1941). Sometimes, studio interference by producers would generate some conflicts when unfinished films would be tampered with without consulting Ford. One such occurrence happened during *The Grapes of Wrath*, when producer Darryl Zanuck, objected to the rather depressing ending that the director had filmed and, as a result, Zanuck shot a more "upbeat" finale, which he tacked onto the ending in order to give audiences some hope.

Behind the Scenes of *They Were Expendable*

A similar event happened on *My Darling Clementine*, with Zanuck (again) shooting a scene of Henry Fonda (as Wyatt Earp) visiting the gravesite of his slain younger brother, who was murdered by the Clantons. Apparently, Zanuck must have loved a similar scene in *Young Mr. Lincoln* with Henry Fonda (as Lincoln) visiting the gravesite of his beloved Ann Rutledge. Also, there were other omissions from and additions to the film, which infuriated Ford.

Nevertheless, his love for America and American history is not only evident in his westerns, but in the three films he made with humorist Will Rogers (*Dr. Bull, Judge Priest, Steamboat 'Round the Bend*) as well as *Pilgrimage* (1933), *The Prisoner of Shark Island* (1936), *Young Mr. Lincoln* (1939) and *Drums Along the Mohawk* (1939). He even delved into more "offbeat" entries, which weren't considered typical Ford works, but were quite good just the same. *The Whole Town's Talking* (1935) was a terrific screwball comedy, which starred Edward G. Robinson, who was spoofing his gangster persona, and Jean Arthur, who became Columbia's biggest female lead after the film was released.

Another oddity was the excellent pre-code offering, *Flesh* (1932), an overlooked little gem, which starred burly Wallace Beery as a dim-witted German wrestler, with Beery turning out one of his best performances (much in the same manner as Emil Jannings in *Der Blau Engel* (The Blue Angel). Ford would also tackle the "disaster craze" of the mid to late thirties with *The Hurricane* (1937), a splendid example of Hollywood special effects in full swing due to the technical expertise of James Basevi.

Of course, like all filmmakers, there were some misfires, most notably *Mary of Scotland* (1936), *Tobacco Road* (1941), *When Willie Comes Marching Home* (1950) and *What Price Glory?* (1952). Perhaps these projects missed their mark because the subject matter was not of particular interest to Ford.

Like most directors, he had favorite actors he loved working with, including John Wayne, Henry Fonda, Maureen O'Hara and later James Stewart, as well as a whole stable of stock players, actors and actresses whom he used frequently and depended on throughout his career. His stock company included Victor McLaglen, Barry Fitzgerald, Harry Carey, Sr. and Jr., Ward Bond, John Carradine, Mae Marsh, Ben Johnson, Jack Pennick, Donald Meek, Una O'Connor and many others whose mere appearance enhanced any film in which they appeared.

I. Overview of the Film and Its Making

Ford Goes to War

In 1939, with the impending war lurking over the horizon, Ford was convinced that the United States would eventually be drawn into the carnage and he convinced Washington of the importance of a motion picture unit to film the struggle firsthand. Given the "go-ahead," he set up the Eleventh Naval District Motion Picture and Still Photographic Group, into which he enlisted more than 200 men who had been working in various areas of the movie industry, and began training them on a weekly basis. The unit would make documentaries and propaganda films to "record the history (progress) of the Navy in World War II." Among some of Ford's recruits were cinematographers Gregg Toland and Joseph August as well as future director Robert Parrish and Ford's "right-hand man," Jack Pennick. The training sessions were usually held at Twentieth Century–Fox or the Naval Reserve Armory in Los Angeles. There were nine divisions in Ford's unit, complete with a camera crew, all willing, able and ready to film documentaries under the most trying and dangerous circumstances, using both 35mm and 16mm equipment.

On September 11, 1941, Ford was inducted in the Navy as a lieutenant commander for the duration of the war. John Wayne tried to join, but was turned down due to his age and an ear infection he had gotten while filming *Reap the Wild Wind* (1942), when doing some very difficult and lengthy underwater scenes with a "giant squid." Also, he had too many "dependents" according to his son and, as a result, was classified as 4-F whenever he tried enlisting. Herbert Yates, the president of Republic Pictures, certainly didn't want to let go of his most successful commodity since Wayne was becoming one of the top box office stars in Hollywood. Yates kept insisting that Wayne could do more for the war effort by making patriotic pro–American war films (Wayne would make quite a few during this time, among them *Flying Tigers, The Fighting Seabees* and *Back to Bataan*). As for Ward Bond, he was excused due to his epilepsy.

Ford didn't believe the Wayne story and kept showing his disapproval in letters to his wife, Mary, who informed him that shortly after Pearl Harbor, both Wayne and Bond took positions as "lookouts" on the California coastline, keeping an eye out for a possible Japanese invasion. Ford's sarcastic reply came in his next letter, "Such heroism shall not go unrewarded. It will live in the annals of our time."

Behind the Scenes of *They Were Expendable*

During World War II, Commander John Ford (USNR) headed the photographic department for the Office of Strategic Services. There, he made five documentaries (*Sex Hygiene, The Battle of Midway, Torpedo Squadron, December 7th* and *We Sail at Midnight*) between the years of 1941 and 1943 (he served in the Navy from 1941 to 1944). He also shot the Navy's raid on Tokyo by the Doolittle Squadron, and filmed the raids on Marcus Island and Wotje and the Normandy landing at Omaha Beach on D-Day. Most of this footage was used in newsreels and for official consumption only.

In early 1942, Japanese Admiral Yamamoto invaded the rather unknown island of Midway, which was located 1,000 miles north of Honolulu. He felt that this would be a decisive battle, which would be the deciding factor of the outcome of the Navy's war in the Pacific. Since Midway was on the perimeter of the Hawaiian waters, there was great concern for our country's safety should Japan be victorious and create a base so close to the western coast of the United States. The Japanese were attempting a surprise attack, but they were unaware that U.S. Intelligence had unraveled their code and thus knew beforehand of the imminent invasion.

Ford and Jack MacKenzie, Jr. (son of Hollywood cameraman Jack MacKenzie) were sent to Midway two weeks before the invasion to cover the battle. Ford was asked by Captain Simard, commander of the Naval Air Station on Midway, to be a forward observer, staying in the ship's powerhouse with his trusty 16mm camera (along with a hefty supply of 16mm Kodachrome film) with two phones at the ready to report the battle's progress to his superior officers.

For a while, things were looking bleak, but eventually the American bombers caught the Japanese aircraft carrier and pounced on it from all directions. Three enemy carriers were sunk in the melee and a fourth was disposed of early the next morning. Yamamoto made a complete "about face" and retreated. This proved to be a debilitating defeat for the Japanese, the first in their Navy's history.

The *Hollywood Reporter* carried the story about Ford filming *The Battle of Midway* and the raw footage was sent to Ford's superior, General William "Wild Bill" Donovan, who claimed "the pictures (Ford) took on Midway are remarkable. I think and believe Jack will be given the Navy Cross as a result of his conduct in the Midway action."

I. Overview of the Film and Its Making

Future director and former actor, Robert Parrish, who worked with Ford on *Midway*, recalled that between 20,000 and 30,000 feet of raw 16mm footage was shot, enough for a feature-length documentary. Ford whittled it down to 16 minutes. Parrish told Lindsay Anderson, for his excellent book *About John Ford*, what it was like working with him. As described by Anderson,

> Ford hi-jacked the eight cans of 16 millimeter material whose shooting he had supervised during the Japanese attack on Midway Island [and] set Parrish to work in secret, editing a picture "for the mothers of America." [Ford] enlisted Dudley Nichols and James Kevin McGuinness (informing neither of the other's participation) to write commentary and lines for [Henry] Fonda, [Jane] Darwell, Irving Pichel and Donald Crisp ... and won the backing of Roosevelt by cutting in a five-foot close-up of his son which he'd been carrying around in his pocket. No, the film is not a documentary classic; yes, it is an extremely skillful (and heart-felt) manipulation of patriotic sentiment. "When the lights came up, Mrs. Roosevelt was crying. The President turned to Admiral Leahy and said, 'I want every mother in America to see this picture.'"

It won the Academy Award for best short subject in 1942. Parrish sums up: "I saw a number of women actually sobbing, and most of them looked like mothers. As usual, Ford achieved his objective" (Anderson, 89).

A few months after the release of *The Battle of Midway*, another John Ford documentary, *December 7th*, premiered and, as author and John Ford scholar Scott Eyman states, it "was one of Ford's great achievements." The *New York Times* review stated, "For eighteen tingling and harshly realistic minutes the spectator is plunged into the front line amid the thunder of exploding bombs, the angry whine of fighter planes locked in combat and the relentless bark of anti-aircraft guns aboard surface vessels."

Preparations for *They Were Expendable*

In April of 1943, Frank Wilbur "Spig" Wead, a former Naval aviator who would advance aviation for the Navy from its very beginnings up through World War II and who would later be the subject of John Ford's venture, *The Wings of Eagles* (1957), approached Ford along with

Behind the Scenes of *They Were Expendable*

screenwriter James Kevin McGuinness to convince him to make a Hollywood-produced movie based on William L. White's book *They Were Expendable*. Wead, who had turned to screenwriting after a tragic accident left him paralyzed, had adapted a scenario based on the novel. It proved to hold more compassion and intensity than White's novel and Wead felt that Ford would be the right man to direct the movie, but ... would Ford accept? Both Wead and McGuinness informed Ford that this undertaking would prove more important than continuing his work for the Field Photographic Unit. Ford was apprehensive at first, claiming that he would be criticized for filming a commercial movie while still in uniform. Still pressuring him into submission, Wead and McGuinness tried convincing him that the movie would aid the war effort significantly and perhaps Ford might donate his salary to the Navy Relief Fund. Ford agreed.

In June of 1943 they were set to begin production when MGM chief Eddie Mannix wanted to bring in writer Sidney Franklin to "polish up the script." Unfortunately, Franklin knew nothing about naval procedures and his "rewrites" proved to be shallow and lifeless. Knowing full well that Metro-Goldwyn-Mayer, which had a reputation for making lightweight musicals and big-budget films based on literary novels, would make a mess of the whole affair, Ford backed out of the production after reading the script and decided to abandon the project and leave on assignment in China and India that August.

Eight months later, while on leave in Los Angeles, Ford was once again plagued with visits from McGuinness, who pleaded with Ford to reconsider his decision and shoot the picture. According to his grandson, Dan Ford, in his excellent biography entitled *Pappy: The Life of John Ford*, McGuinness argued, "this isn't another war movie. The story of John Bulkeley and his PT squadron is part of America's heroic tradition.... It will be available for our youth, generation after generation." Even with this, Ford stayed pat on his decision and told McGuinness that he was committed to a major operation, ... "one that would probably decide the outcome of the war. Your film will have to wait." McGuinness then pressed him, "But we've got no picture without you!" "Tell that to Eddie Mannix!" growled Ford. Another factor that convinced Ford to resume his career in the Navy was the fact that his documentary, *December 7th*, had won an Academy Award, his fourth.

On April 5, 1944, Ford was promoted to captain and was soon transported to London on a military plane to cover the Normandy invasion

I. Overview of the Film and Its Making

with his film crew. Mark Armistead, who was a young recruit with the Field Photographic Unit, was assigned a team of men to photograph the European coastline from low-flying B-25s to collect information and to interview local residents who knew the area well. It was at this time that Ford met Lt. John Bulkeley, the man who had evacuated Gen. Douglas MacArthur out of the Philippines. Ford was very familiar with Bulkeley's exploits and was impressed that he knew these waters like the back of his hand since he had been running agents and officials in and out of Normandy.

Ford was honored to meet Bulkeley, who downplayed his heroism by telling Ford that he had hoped that MGM wouldn't make a film based on his naval record. This modesty really impressed Ford and as their friendship grew, Ford decided that *They Were Expendable* should be a priority as soon as he returned to Hollywood.

Previously, Ford had made two excellent war-related films while in Hollywood: *Four Sons* (1928) and especially *The Lost Patrol* (1934), the theme of which has been reworked/remade many times, most notably in films like *Bataan* and *Sahara* (1943). *They Were Expendable*, which was based on a best-selling non-fiction account by William White, was a book about the heroic feats aboard a squadron of PT boats battling the Japanese and later evacuating Gen. Douglas MacArthur from the Philippines. Based upon interviews with Lieutenant Bulkeley, who was later awarded the Congressional Medal of Honor, the book became a national bestseller and is still in print today.

Ford first reported to the USS *Augusta* on June 5, 1944, readying for the Normandy invasion with its 4,600 ships and 176,000 men. He initially observed the actual battle through binoculars at a safe distance. Becoming rather bored by witnessing the whole account from so far away, he radioed Mark Armistad, who was on Bulkeley's PT boat, indicating that he wanted part of the action. Bulkeley readily conceded to his request, pulled up next to the *Augusta* and picked up Ford and welcomed him aboard.

Ford did see plenty of action when a group of German E-boats engaged in a machine gun duel with Bulkeley and his crew. Ford was rather amused that he was involved in the Normandy Invasion with the man who would be the subject of his first Hollywood film after he returned to civilian life. Ford always said that he greatly admired the lieutenant and how professionally he conducted himself under any circumstance and how modest he was in real life. After observing first-hand what a great commander Bulkeley was, Ford had come to realize that McGuinness and Wead were right in their assessment of the man. Now, it was time to return to Hollywood and begin plans for the picture.

Secretary of the Navy James Forrestal wrote the director of the Office of Strategic Services (OSS) on September 12, 1944, that MGM had requested Commander John Ford to direct a Hollywood-produced picture and that "this picture would be helpful to the Navy, and because Commander Ford is ably qualified by reason of his motion picture experience and his naval experience, I hope that he will be made available."

The first thing Ford did upon returning home was to contact James McGuinness and Frank "Spig" Wead to once again flesh out the script. According to film historian Jeffry Heise, Wead's script opened with Brickley and "Rusty" Ryan flying out of the Philippines to the United States ... then, in flashback, it shows the PT boats arriving days before the attack on Pearl Harbor, all narrated by Brickley (Robert Montgomery). Also, there was to be more footage of the Donna Reed character as well.

A later draft by Frank Wead, dated September 1, 1944, had "Rusty" (Wayne) returning to the Philippines at the conclusion of the movie to find that Peggy (Reed) is alive. It was a happy ending to be sure, but a scene that undoubtedly was nixed by Ford. Before production could begin, Ford had to receive permission from his home studio, Twentieth Century–Fox, to be loaned to MGM. Studio head Darryl F. Zanuck agreed and it looked like the making of *They Were Expendable* would become a reality. Ford willingly agreed because of the $300,000 fee he was promised and also because of the film's subject matter.

Even though Ford would express in later life that he never wanted to make the film, he did say to his wife in a letter that he was excited to begin the project and the entire cast, all of whom were waiting for filming to commence, were growing beards and getting tans in the blazing sun. Ford also noted that he was amused at seeing all of the women who visited the location "swooning" over John Wayne and Ward Bond. Bond, in particular, amused (or annoyed) Ford, who called him a "pain in the ass" because of his blustery demeanor and his tremendous ego.

In Tag Gallagher's study, *John Ford: The Man and His Films*, Ford related,

> What I had in mind was doing it (*They Were Expendable*) exactly as it had happened. It was strange to do this picture about Johnny Bulkeley.... I knew him so well. He was the fellow in Guantanamo who,

I. Overview of the Film and Its Making

when Castro cut the lines off, quickly installed the water system. During the (world) war, my district was around Bayeux, practically on the Coast, and it was pretty well populated with the SS and Gestapo. So instead of dropping an agent in, we took a PT boat, which Johnny always skippered himself ... he refused to let me go in unless he skippered the ship. We used to go back and forth ... we could always slip in there, if the signals were right ... because the Resistance had told us the Germans never thought of guarding this one creek. We'd go in there on one engine, drop an agent off or pick up information, and disappear [221].

When *They Were Expendable* was in its earliest stages, MGM producer James McGuinness emphasized the point that he didn't want to make just "another war picture." He stated, "The story of the expendables seems to me as much a part of America's heroic tradition as the Alamo, the Green Mountain Boys at Ticonderoga, Valley Forge, or any of the great patriotic heroics of our national life." He also insisted that they rush into production as soon as possible while it "was still fresh in the minds of those who lived it." Ford stood in total agreement with the producer, feeling that he didn't want this to be another "blood and guts, flag-waving propaganda film." An honest account was what they had in mind.

Ford was obsessed with making *They Were Expendable* a stand-out film, realistic enough to pay tribute to the heroes upon whom the story was based. He even brought his "right-hand man" Jack Pennick and his men from the Field Photographic Unit to work as extras to add some realism. He wanted the production to include his own personal experiences while in the Navy. According to author Tag Gallagher, Ford wanted this film to be a dedication to the "little men who see only the war in front of them, and rarely see even that. No Japanese are seen; the struggle is interiorized. Only the evacuation of MacArthur—not even the battles—takes on dimensions of an event, and this for the man's symbolic value, rather than for the trip itself, which Ford eludes. And so much is in the emphasis on the group, not on the individual" (223).

Robert Montgomery had been serving in the Navy for about four years when Ford asked him if he'd like to play a character based on Lt. Bulkeley in his upcoming film. People were surprised when Ford cast him in the part, but the persistent director thought he would be perfect because he had commanded a fleet of PT boats in the Solomon Islands. For years before the war, while under contract to MGM, Montgomery struggled to receive good parts, but always seemed to be cast as rich playboys in top hat and tuxedo in rather lackluster roles.

Ford convinced navy officials to release Montgomery from active service after a stellar wartime record, which included being a first assistant U.S. naval attaché in London, serving aboard a destroyer during the D-Day invasion and being awarded the Bronze Star and a Chevalier of the French Legion of Honor. As far as Ford was concerned, Montgomery had "earned the right" to portray a navy hero.

Shooting on Location

With Ford in the director's chair, Bob Montgomery knew that this would be a golden opportunity for him. Unfortunately, when the time came to start shooting the picture, Montgomery became rather panic-stricken because he thought that he had forgotten how to perform in front of a camera. When he confided to Ford about his fears, the director was very patient and understanding and suggested to Montgomery that he go "take the boats out and run them around" for relaxation until he felt that he was ready.

After three days of observing Ford directing other scenes and working the whole company around his absence, Montgomery felt that he was ready enough and informed Ford. In retrospect, Bob Montgomery's performance is so natural, so restrained, that it can go unnoticed by critics and audiences. It just proves what a good actor he really was when given the opportunity.

Location shooting commenced on February 1, 1945, in Miami (not on Key Biscayne as earlier documents and film historians have stated). When filming began, it seemed that the war was far from over. Fighting was still raging in the Pacific. Gen. Douglas MacArthur had fled Bataan and Corregidor and by the time shooting began, Allied forces were trying to recapture both of them. American troops had just raised their flag atop Mount Suribachi in Iwo Jima. However, it seemed that there would be still much fighting in the months ahead.

The Navy loaned MGM several squadrons of PT boats and Capt. Jim Havens of the Marines was brought in as a second unit director to photograph many of the battle scenes back in Culver City, California. The actual

I. Overview of the Film and Its Making

Montgomery and Wayne in another posed publicity shot, manning the P.T. boat (courtesy of John McElwee).

locations were off the Miami coastline as well as on an uninhabited island nearby, which usually took the cast and crew approximately 20 minutes to reach from Florida's shore. Once shooting began, Ford took control in his usual harsh manner, constantly changing and eliminating certain bits from the script.

    According to Robert Montgomery, one such instance occurred while they were filming the scene where a young submarine officer, Ensign "Snake" Gardner, played by Marshall Thompson, extorts some torpedoes from Wayne and Montgomery's characters. Originally, there were pages and pages of dialogue for Thompson to memorize. He came on the set one morning fully prepared to give his long speech, when Ford marched over to him, gave him one sheet of paper with about four lines scribbled on it and said, "This is all you say in this scene" and walked back to his chair, leaving the poor young actor scratching his head in disbelief.

One obstacle that needed to be overcome was the fact that Ward Bond was involved in a car accident just prior to shooting, which resulted in a broken foot. All during the filming, they had to shoot Bond from the waist up and if they needed a shot of him walking, they had to film the take, shooting from behind, utilizing a stand-in. Later, some "on set inspiration" by Ford had Bond's character, "Boats" Mulcahey, getting wounded, so his foot injury comes into play in the finished product.

John Wayne's character of Lt. j.g. "Rusty" Ryan was based on Commander Robert B. Kelly, U.S.N., who became an instructor at the Naval Academy at Annapolis after the war. During the war, Kelly was executive officer for Lt. John D. Bulkeley during the evacuation of Gen. Douglas MacArthur from Corregidor. Later on, he commanded a destroyer.

While *They Were Expendable* was in general release, Commander Robert Kelly sued Loew's Inc. for $50,000 (see Appendix), claiming that his reputation among fellow officers was injured by the portrayal of him as "Rusty" Ryan in the picture. Kelly objected to the fact that Ryan was a strong-willed individual who at times questions authority and seems to lead his men through his own instincts, something that is not in the line with the personality of an officer. Even at the end of the film, when Ryan and Brickley board a transport plane that has limited seating for the other sailors who are to evacuate the Philippines, Rusty attempts to sacrifice his own seat, but is quickly admonished by "Brick," who asks "Rusty, who are you working for ... yourself?" Judge Charles E. Wyzanski, Jr., heard the case in Federal Court and decided in Kelly's behalf, demanding that the studio pay him $3,000 in damages.

As previously noted, since John Wayne was not in the military due to his age, Ford always seemed to take delight in berating him. Though it certainly wasn't Wayne's fault, Ford would exclude him from any conversations between takes when military officers and other dignitaries would visit the set. Years later, Wayne would relate, "Jack was awfully intense on that picture and working with more concentration than I had ever seen. I think he was really out to achieve something." He went on to say, "Bob Montgomery was his pet on that picture. He could do no wrong. I guess it was because he had been in the navy. Jack picked on me all the way through it."

I. Overview of the Film and Its Making

Wayne told Dan Ford, "We almost got into a fistfight at one point. It was while we were shooting a process scene where my boat is strafed by an airplane. A special effects guy was shooting ball bearings at my boat, and he had forgotten to replace the windshield with a non-breakable plexiglass one. Real glass went flying into my face. In a rage I grabbed a hammer and went after the guy. But Jack stepped in front of me and said, 'No you don't. They're my crew.' 'Your crew, goddammit, they're my eyes,' I said" (Ford, 200).

Ford would continue his needling of Wayne, often calling him a "big oaf" and a "clumsy bastard." On one occasion, he kept making Robert Montgomery and "Duke" Wayne do a scene over and over where the two of them had to salute some superior officers. A simple take like this should have been no problem, but Ford kept insisting that they do retake after retake. Finally, Wayne whispered to Montgomery, asking what they could possibly be doing wrong? Suddenly, Ford burst out of his chair and marched over to Wayne and yelled at him, "For Christ sake, Duke, can't you salute someone in the proper manner?" By the time Ford returned to his seat, it was evident that he had humiliated Wayne in front of the entire company. Realizing this, Montgomery had had enough and walked over to Ford and admonished him by saying, "Don't ever talk to Duke like that! You ought to be ashamed."

As Montgomery went back to take his position before the camera, he turned around to see the director's reaction when he noticed that Ford had been quite shaken up. Ford, who truly felt that they had a father/son relationship throughout their careers, had always treated Wayne like a naughty child who had just misbehaved, and this was no exception. Wayne and others had learned to accept this on-set behavior amiably because they knew that Ford was a strict taskmaster who knew what was right for the picture.

Claire Trevor, who co-starred with Duke in *Stagecoach*, recalled that whenever Wayne messed up a take, Ford would make him get down on all fours in front of the whole company, sit on his back, and push his face into the mud. Ward Bond would also take the brunt of Ford's abuse, as he constantly made fun of Ward's rather large posterior. One time, he invited Bond into the screening room to watch the previous day's "rushes." To Bond's horror, every shot taken was a close-up of Ward's rather ample derriere, which delighted Ford, who was laughing uncontrollably. Another time, Ford had a picture taken of himself and Wayne standing on either side of the rear end of a horse. Ford sent the photo to Bond with the inscription, "Thinking of you...."

When Ward Bond died unexpectedly of a massive heart attack in 1960, Ford walked over to comedy veteran Andy Devine, who was next in line as one of his "victims," and said to him, "Now that Ward's gone, you're now the biggest asshole I know!" Saying that he could be abusive was certainly an understatement, but all of the cast and crew knew that whatever Ford did would turn into cinematic gold on the screen.

Winding Up Production

Location shooting on the small, uncharted island and the coast of Miami had lasted 30 days. That left all of the scenes with the female members of the cast as well as the battle scenes with all of their technical special effects wizardry to be shot at MGM in Culver City. Resuming shooting on May 14 at the studio, Ford proved to be just as abusive to his leading lady, Donna Reed, as he had been to Duke Wayne. Apparently, one day before shooting was to resume, the wardrobe department had brought Ms. Reed over to the director, asking him to inspect her costume for the picture for approval. When she came over to Ford to ask for his opinion, he growled and said, "Nobody gives a damn what you're wearing in a picture like this!"

According to Robert Montgomery, Donna Reed was "very intelligent and she didn't let Ford upset her: she used his attitude ... played off it. It gave her strength. And she gave a fine performance. After we'd been working with her about three weeks, I (Robert Montgomery) took her across the floor and presented her to Ford. I said: 'I think it's time you were introduced to our director.' He took it very well: they got on fine after that" (McBride, 407). Ford later presented Reed with a necklace during filming.

In Lindsay Anderson's excellent study of John Ford, entitled *About John Ford*, the author relates that Ford didn't like *They Were Expendable* (not true) because he was forced to make it. Not only that, integral scenes were totally eliminated prior to its release. He also balked at the idea of being pulled away from active duty to direct a picture where some of the more temperamental actors refused to get their hair cut in order to look like real Navy men. According to Ford, he had never even seen the final cut and when years later, John Wayne told Ford that he had recently screened a print of the film and said how great he thought it was, Ford felt that Wayne was just being nice.

I. Overview of the Film and Its Making

One more conflict arose towards the end of the film's production. It has been said that Ford wanted no music in *They Were Expendable*, except perhaps "Red River Valley" in the scene with Russell Simpson. MGM insisted that background music was necessary, and MGM studio composer Herbert Stothart was drafted to compose the score. Although his previous efforts tended to be rather melodramatic, featuring the muted chords of violins, as in *Waterloo Bridge* (1940) and *Random Harvest* (1942), he did an outstanding job with his evocative score, much in the Ford tradition (how much of the score Ford suggested is a matter of conjecture). Stothart did use some classic tunes like "The Battle Hymn of the Republic" and "Anchors Aweigh" to placate the patriotic director.

The remainder of the shoot apparently went quite well, until Ford tripped on some cables between two cameras (some accounts claim he fell 20 feet from a scaffold). John Wayne saw a chance to get even with the director, yelling, "Jesus Christ, you clumsy bastard!" When Ford was taken to the hospital by John Wayne and Ward Bond following the accident, the three of them were in the hospital elevator and in walked a woman who just kept staring at Ford in his wheelchair. Ford blurted "Alcohol," which prompted the woman to leave the elevator in a huff.

Ford only had one more scene left to shoot along with some 2nd unit work. While recuperating in Cedars of Lebanon Hospital with a compound fracture in his leg for two weeks, Ford relegated the task of directing the remainder of the picture to Bob Montgomery. During his stay in the hospital, Ford was able to reflect on the four years he spent with the Field Photographic Unit and years later, he would call these the most fulfilling years of his life.

Agreeing to this new undertaking, Montgomery really took to directing, although many times he had to hold his tongue when it came to dealing with Ward Bond, whom Montgomery had come to dislike intensely. Bond, who was a favorite of Ford's, was frequently disagreeable and boisterous, which always amused the director, but frustrated the amiable Montgomery. Bond used to act like he was the star of the film and would endlessly try to bed every starlet when they returned to Culver City to shoot many of the interior scenes.

To ease the tension between the two, Wayne and Montgomery thought up an elaborate practical joke to play on Bond. Since Montgomery was always being invited to important military parties, he let it slip ("accidentally

Behind the Scenes of *They Were Expendable*

Wayne, Donna Reed and Montgomery posing in front of a "process screen" for publicity taken at MGM Studios in Culver City (courtesy of John McElwee).

on purpose," with Ward Bond within hearing distance) that he had been invited to a formal affair for the British royalty in the Bahamas. After a while, it became known that John Ford and John Wayne were also invited and Wayne kept talking about how excited and honored he was that he had been included. At one point, Wayne even asked Ward if he could borrow his white dinner jacket for the affair. Never one who liked to be left out, Bond fumed and fumed until it was later revealed that the whole thing was merely a joke played on him by his "pals."

In later years, Bob Montgomery would recall how impressed he was with Ford's crew of technicians, relating how professional everyone was and how they all knew exactly what they were doing, without anyone breathing down their necks. Montgomery would also state that John Ford was the best

I. Overview of the Film and Its Making

director he had ever worked with and he would have signed a contract to work for him exclusively if the subject ever came up, which it didn't. The actor knew that this was one of his best acting jobs ever and he gave a performance that was authentic and never overplayed his part, keeping within the realms of a reserved commander whose devotion to his men and, above all, duty, are the most important characteristics to this modest hero.

Working on *They Were Expendable* turned out to be a major turning point in the actor's movie career and he obviously enjoyed the experience, so much so that he immediately began directing, turning out two good film noir dramas in quick succession, which he also starred in: *Lady in the Lake* (1946) and *Ride the Pink Horse* (1947), as well as films like *The Gallant Hours* (1960) with his good pal James Cagney, and some television work.

In 1980, Robert Montgomery, in an interview with Lindsay Anderson, said, "Anything that's good about *They Were Expendable*, in the script, the performance, the editing, the camerawork, was Ford's achievement. He'd done a lot of rewriting on the script MGM had produced: there was a lot of bad stuff in it. He got Frank Wead in and they did it together. Then during shooting he was making changes all the time. Sometimes he'd expand a few lines into a page of dialogue. And sometimes he'd take pages of dialogue and reduce them to a few lines." Montgomery went on to say that sometimes they would rehearse a scene while other times, they would "do it straight off." The scene where Montgomery says goodbye to his men who are to join the army on Bataan was done in one take.

The War in the Pacific ended with the bombings of Hiroshima and Nagasaki on August 15, while *They Were Expendable* was still in post-production. On September 2, Gen. Douglas MacArthur accepted Japan's surrender. World War II had ended and Ford was called into Gen. Bill Donovan's office and was presented with the Legion of Merit. The following day, the Field Photographic Unit disbanded and its commanding officer was once again a civilian.

Release and Reception

MGM had planned to release *They Were Expendable* in September of 1945 and anticipated that it would be viewed by a nation still at war, but because of the Japanese surrender its release was delayed. When the movie premiered on December 20, 1945, America was already celebrating victories over Germany and Japan. MGM heralded the picture as "one of the greatest films of our time." The movie received rave reviews although some sources claim that audiences stayed away in droves because they had tired of "war pictures." That statement actually proved false because the film eventually became one of the top grossing films of 1945–1946 along with such blockbusters as *The Bells of St. Mary's, Gilda, Leave Her to Heaven, The Lost Weekend, Mildred Pierce, Notorious, Spellbound, Weekend at the Waldorf*, and others.

When the movie premiered, critics lauded it as "a labor of understanding and love" and called it an "enthralling tribute." Initially, the film didn't do too well at the box office, but it steadily gained momentum in the ensuing months, eventually making it to number 29 in the top moneymakers of 1945. Critic Bosley Crowther noted that "it is in no way depreciatory of ... *They Were Expendable* to say that if this film had been released last year, or the year before, it would have been a ringing smash. Now, with the war concluded and the burning thirst for vengeance somewhat cooled, it comes as a cinematic postscript to the martial heat and passion of the last four years." John Wayne added that "after eight million war stories, people were tired of them." This statement was verified by the fact that the biggest grossing film of the year was Leo McCarey's *The Bells of St. Mary's*. Nevertheless, *They Were Expendable* would gross $4.1 million worldwide against costs of $2.9 million, still an impressive figure for its time.

Critic James Agee wrote, "For what seems at least half of its dogged, devoted length, all you have to watch is men getting on and off PT boats and other men watching them do so. But this is made so beautiful and so real that I could not feel one foot of the film was wasted."

Although *They Were Expendable* wasn't nominated for Best Picture of 1945, it was nominated for Best Sound Recording (by Douglas Shearer, who lost to Stephen Dunn for *The Bells of St. Mary's*) and Best Special Effects (by Arnold Gillespie, Donald Jahraus, R.A. MacDonald and Michael Steinore, losing to John Fulton and A.W. Johns for *Wonder Man*). Even though it came up empty in the two Academy Award categories, this John Ford masterpiece remains one of the best war movies ever made and gives a realistic account of war, patriotism and bravery.

Rather than donating his salary to the Navy Relief, Ford decided to buy land and build a clubhouse for the men of the Field Photographic Unit as a

I. Overview of the Film and Its Making

John Wayne and Robert Montgomery ask Eve March if they may visit their dying friend in the makeshift naval hospital (courtesy of John McElwee).

"living memorial" to his men and their unit. He found a 20-acre estate in the San Fernando Valley and built the structure for his men and their families for an estimated cost of $225,000. John Wayne even donated $10,000. The clubhouse was located at 18201 Calvert Street in Resada and was fully equipped with a well-stocked bar, swimming pool, tennis courts and baseball field where the men and their families could relax and spend some quality time together.

II: THE PHOTOGRAPHER

An Interview with Nick Scutti

Born January 23, 1926, in Stamford, Connecticut, Nick Scutti always was interested in photography. Following high school, Nick enlisted in the U.S. Navy and was sworn in October 1, 1943. His passion for photography led him to a position with the Sub Chaser Training Center in Miami, Florida. While in training, he eventually was involved with the Central Issuing Office working in the photo lab, studying nights and learning all about cameras and photography and eventually volunteering in all photographic events. In late 1944, director John Ford called the naval office and informed them that MGM would be sending a film crew to shoot the upcoming wartime film They Were Expendable. *As a captain in the U.S. Navy, Ford invited the men from the naval lab to come to the set on a daily basis. Nick had the wherewithal to bring his camera and began shooting photographs of the entire location shoot, which lasted 30 days.*

After his stint with the navy, Nick returned to his hometown, and resumed his schooling in photography through the GI Bill and went into business for himself, freelancing and eventually becoming a professional photographer. Some of the more famous celebrities Nick has photographed through the years include Mickey Mantle, Roger Maris, Ingrid Bergman, Albert Einstein, Ted Williams and Joe DiMaggio, many of whom were included in various books with which Nick had been involved. Married in 1954 to Ann Masotta, they enjoyed 55 years of happily married life until her death in 2008. Today, Nick is happily retired and has three sons, Paul, James and Steven, as well as three grandchildren.

II. The Photographer

LS: Well first of all, thank you for letting me do this interview with you, Nick. How did you become interested in photography?

NS: Okay, let's start when I was about age seven. I liked recording things and I liked to keep a record of everything that I had seen and the only way to do it was through photography. But, at the time, I was unable to buy a camera. Remember, I was one of six children and my mother and father held two or three jobs to keep us six going and they couldn't afford to buy me a camera. So, I heard about a company that was offering a free camera, if you sold a number of chances on a prize that they gave. They called it a candid camera and the way I was to obtain one of these was to sell these cards to prospective customers. They were similar to today's daily lottery "scratch-offs."

Anyway, I was one of the winners of that contest and I won the camera, which turned out to be one of the cheapest cameras you've ever seen. I don't think it was worth $5. But, I enjoyed using it and I was happy to get it. That's how my interest in photography began.

Why did you enlist in the Navy?

My uncle Ralph Scutti had been in the Navy in the early 30s and he was a chief petty officer, a signalman and I also had a cousin, Nick Scutti (same name) who was in the Navy in 1940. He was there when World War II broke out. Getting back to my Uncle Ralph, he was at Pearl Harbor when it was bombed by the Japanese. So after seeing my uncle and my cousin in the navy, I thought I would follow in their footsteps because I always was interested in their naval careers because I respected everything they did. That was one of the main reasons why I wanted to be in the Navy.

Tell me a little about your naval career.

That started on October 1, 1943, and I was to report to New Haven to be sworn in and at that time I assumed I was going to be sent somewhere for naval training, but that didn't happen because at the time there was a surplus of men who were joining the Navy and they had no room in their training center in Sampson, New York. Finally, later on in January of 1944, I went up to Sampson for some hasty training, which was supposed to take eight weeks … but there were so many guys joining they didn't have room for us and training only took three weeks.

Between these portals pass the best damn photographers - - - - in the world - -

II. The Photographer

Tell me about the Sub Chaser Training Center (their function) in Miami, Florida. How did you become involved with it?

After my training at Sampson, we were sent to Miami to the Sub Chaser Training Center and the site was located in the center of town and they had three piers there right off the shore. The three piers were taken over by the navy and then they converted a large warehouse into a school with school rooms where we would watch slides and receive more training. Later, some of the men were sent on destroyers, minesweepers or torpedo boats after they were fully trained.

Were you already considered a professional photographer by this time?

No, by no means. I was just considered an amateur.

What was your job with the Sub Chaser Center?

Well, actually my job wasn't really considered a job, it was more of an assignment to transport high octane gasoline from island to island in the Pacific.

So, were you involved in any other activities with the Navy? Were you sent overseas and did you see any action?

Well, before going overseas we had to go through this training period and we were assigned on a tanker where we were taught how to survive if we were to get hit by a torpedo. After about eight weeks, we were sent to another ship, an oil tanker, where we were supposed to board it at the naval base in Norfolk, Virginia. From there we were sent to the Brooklyn Navy Yard.

Since we were on a firefighting ship, we were then put into firefighting school, which was the toughest thing I did while in the navy. After that, they sent me south again and en route to Miami, I got some kind of infection, which triggered a high temperature of 104 so they pulled into shore and sent me back to the hospital in Miami and I was there for about three weeks. Eventually, they got me all better and in the meantime, our ship had to leave to continue on a shakedown cruise and I was left behind due to my illness.

By coincidence, my uncle in Connecticut had a brother living in Coral Gables, Florida, and I got in touch with him and he invited me over for dinner on a Sunday afternoon. At dinner, I met a naval man named Hatfield

Opposite: **Photographer Nick Scutti at the Naval Photographic Lab, ca. 1944.**

and he was a petty officer first class and asked me what I was doing down in Miami, where I was stationed, etc. I told him that I was in a "pool" awaiting further instructions. He then inquired what I wanted to do and I told him that I would like to get into photography if I could. He told me he worked for the officer in charge of photography, printing and public relations and he said he would see what he could do for me. Of course, I didn't believe anything would come of this.

The following day, my name was called on the loud speaker to report to a certain officer, who talked to me about my love for photography. He asked if I would be interested in working in the lab and told me to go see Joe Maddock, who was a first class photographer's mate. He went on to say that if Joe could use me, he could teach me the ropes. Upon meeting Joe, he asked me how much I knew about photography and I told him "not too much, but I'm willing to learn." Lying on the center of the table between us, there was a camera and he asked if I knew what a Speed Graphic was and as I fumbled, trying to find my words, Joe pointed to the camera and said "That's a Speed Graphic." I looked at Joe and asked in embarrassment, "Where's the door?" At that point, he said that he needed somebody for four months and I assured him that I would be an avid student and would take learning photography diligently.

As it turned out, my job was to make thousands of large prints (20" × 24") with letters of the alphabet (e.g., A is for apple, B is for boy, etc.) and he told me that it would take four months to make these and they would be used for training in the Sub Chaser Training Center for Russian and Chinese sailors who were learning how to read and speak English. The reason for this was due to the fact that some of these sailors were aboard our ships and they had to read signs like "Danger" or "Life Jackets Stored Here" as safety precautions. During those four months, I was off evenings and weekends where I would spend all of my spare time in the library studying every aspect of photography. Actually, that was where I got to learn about photography, by reading and studying and experimenting with my camera. After a couple of months, I got pretty good at it and I kept volunteering to take photos at night and on weekends around our base, nearby Hollywood and Fort Lauderdale.

How did you first hear about John Ford and his crew coming to Miami to film* They Were Expendable*?

We had no idea that this was going to happen. Our officer in charge

II. The Photographer

informed Joe Maddock that they were going to do some filming of the movie *They Were Expendable* in Miami and that only two people who worked in the lab could come up to the filming every day of the shoot and that's how we heard about it. When they asked who wanted to volunteer to see the actually shooting of a Hollywood picture, I immediately volunteered and I was one of the people they selected, probably because I was always volunteering to keep myself busy and this was considered a reward of some sort.

Were you there every day for the entire 30-day shoot?

Yes, I was, and I enjoyed every bit of it. We went out every day to a little island, which we called the Coconut Island. It was uncharted and had no name. We would pile into the PT boats with John Ford and the stars like John Wayne and Robert Montgomery, each engineering their own boats. For fun, they would race each other to the island trying to cause significant wakes in the water to make each other's boats rock, making it more difficult to maneuver. As they would pass the other, they would smile and wave as if they had just won a race to the island.

So, these photographs you took of the filming weren't considered work, correct? It was more recreation?

No, this wasn't work. This was strictly a fun thing for me. You've got to remember that I was only ten or eleven years old when I would go to the movies in my hometown of Stamford, Connecticut, and see both John Wayne and Robert Montgomery up there on that movie screen. I never dreamed that I would actually be seeing them in person and to be actually thrown in with them. It was really something.

Why did you feel the need to document the shooting of the film?

I didn't think anything about documenting.... I just wanted to take these pictures so that my family and friends back home would see what I was doing with these stars because I'm sure they would have been as thrilled as I was just to hear the fact that I was out there with them.

During the 30-day shoot, what did a normal day consist of? When during the day did you go to the location?

Well, we started off the shore in Miami around 9:30 a.m. where the PT boats were docked ... actually it was only three blocks from where I was stationed at the Sub Chaser Training Station. We boarded the boats and it took about twenty minutes to get out to the uninhabited island. This island had no name but there was an abundance of coconuts there and various boats would come in and pick up the coconuts and bring them back to Miami and sell them.

Once we would get to our destination, the camera crews and technicians would get off the boats and go into a huddle for about an hour and after that nobody had to tell them what to do. They all knew exactly where to set the cameras up along with the lights and boom microphone, etc. After everything was set up, the actors would come onto the set and go into another huddle with John Ford, where they would go over their lines and then after a while they would have one "run-through" without the cameras.

After Ford gave them their instructions and he liked what he saw, he would give them the "okay" to start shooting. The soundman would go up on a ladder, blow a whistle, which was a signal for everyone to be quiet and the cameras would begin rolling. Once in a while they would do a retake or a partial retake if Ford wasn't pleased with whatever they had just filmed. There were very, very few retakes because, like I said, these guys were very professional and knew exactly what Ford was looking for and they certainly gave him what he wanted.

Did they shoot any interior scenes or were they just doing exteriors?

They only shot exterior scenes on location and, as I understand it, all interior scenes were filmed in Hollywood. They chose that island to simulate the Philippines where all of the action actually took place.

Where did the cast and crew bunk?

Actually, I did not know exactly where the cast and crew were staying, but I had heard through the grapevine that it was at the Roney Plaza in Miami Beach.

Were there structures for the actors to hang out in between takes?

There were no places to "hang out." We just stood around and the actors would sit anywhere to rest. There were no organized locations to take a breather from filming except for an occasional folding chair.

What about make-up?

I saw one make-up man working on Ward Bond's "stand-in" where he was trying to make him look more like Ward Bond. Mind you, Ward Bond

II. The Photographer

had a broken leg, which he had gotten in an accident before filming began and they used the "stand-in" to do the walking for Bond, which was shot from behind, of course. Now, since this was Florida and it was extremely hot and humid, the make-up man would have to put "sweat marks" on the stand-in's back to match those on Ward Bond. The final result was that you couldn't tell the difference from behind who the real Ward Bond was!

Was there much preparation before they shot a scene?

Not really. It seemed that the stagehands and set designers were out there ready for the actors to come onto the set with the director and they would just be waiting to carry out Ford's instructions.

What was the atmosphere like? Was it a "friendly" set?

Oh yes. It seemed like it was "one big, happy family" like they say. We became like old friends and after 30 days, we were on a first-name basis with some of the stars and crew.

What were your lunch breaks like? Were you able to mingle with the actors? Any good stories about them?

One good story I have to share was one incident involving John Wayne and Ward Bond on the first day of filming during a lunch break. They had just finished their lunches and the two of them were sitting in director's chairs opposite one another, about six feet apart and I happened along and the first one I came to was Ward Bond and I asked him if it would be all right for me to take his picture. Without even looking at me, he said, "No, get outta here! We're having lunch! Don't bother us!" And John Wayne chimed in and said, "C'mon Ward … let the kid take your picture" and reassured me that it would be fine. So, Wayne obligingly turned his chair to face the camera and Bond wouldn't even look in my direction. We took two pictures of this incident and in the second shot, Bond covered his head with his arms.

The next day after lunch, I was walking with a buddy of mine and we saw a shirtless Ward Bond walking our way and I tried to avoid even looking at him when he yelled, "Hey sailor, do you want to take that picture of me now?" I handed my camera to my buddy and he shot this great photo of Ward Bond with yours truly. After that, he seemed like he was a friendly guy. You have to remember, someone who is working in those uncomfortable conditions with all that heat, must get somewhat irritable, especially when he's hobbling around with a broken ankle and a huge cast. It must have been tough for him.

Behind the Scenes of *They Were Expendable*

Another story that occurred during one lunch break had all of us waiting in line to pick up our lunch boxes. I would always let the officers and the movie actors and technicians go ahead of me. But, this one day, after I had assumed that I was one of the last people in line, I happened to turn around and behind me three back was Robert Montgomery and I quickly offered him my place in the "chow" line. He declined my offer to let him go ahead of me and said, "No, thanks, son.... We're all equal here." I couldn't believe my ears because he was an actual commander in the navy and we all looked up to him and after that, I thought a helluva lot of him. He really was a quiet, nice guy, a gentleman.

How long were these lunch breaks? Was everyone served the same food?

They lasted about an hour. We were served a boxed lunch with fruit, usually an apple, a sandwich along with carrots and celery. Everybody, including the actors ate the same thing, Now, I don't know about John Ford, who was usually with naval officers or other dignitaries eating somewhere else.

Did anybody from the Metro-Goldwyn-Mayer Studios show up on the set to consult with Ford?

There were people continuously talking to Ford between scenes and I know that there were many high ranking visitors from the army and navy.

Were there any makeshift dressing rooms for the actors?

No, there were no dressing rooms and I would assume that they would leave their hotel in full costume and someone would drive them down to the pier and then we'd board the boats and go out to the location.

Any funny stories to share during the filming?

Well, normally everybody was pretty serious, but on one particular day, one of Ford's assistants had a birthday ... they didn't have a birthday cake or anything for him, but a bunch of guys grabbed and de-pantsed him and tore his shirt off leaving him standing there in his underwear and socks with the old-fashioned garter belts! We all laughed.... He was quite the sight!

Tell me about character actor Murray Alper. You took two great shots of him that are in the book.

Murray was quite a character. He was always friendly and smiling all

II. The Photographer

the time. I got a hold of him during one of his breaks and he was horsing around with a fake gun when I happened by and asked if I could get a picture. He pulled out the gun and rested it over one of his arms and pointed it at me and gave me a big smile after I took the photos.

Did John Ford offer any specific direction to the actors during filming?

Oh yes…. He was constantly giving directions and if he saw one little thing that he didn't like during their "dry run," he would correct it and tell them what he had changed in the script then give them instructions on what he wanted them to do. This happened very often.

I've always heard from other sources that Robert Montgomery could be rather stand-offish at times. What was your opinion of him?

I thought he was one of the nicest guys on the set. He was very quiet and, for the most part, kept to himself, but never would I say that he was "stand-offish." He would talk a lot with John Wayne or John Ford, probably about what they were going to do in the next scene. He was a very nice guy…. As a matter of fact, I think I would rate him as number one on the set.

And how about John Wayne?

John Wayne? Oh, well … now he was in a special category…. Friendly, happy, smiling, cooperative. Whenever people would visit the location, some of them would come over to me and ask if they could have a picture with John Wayne and I would ask him if it would be all right. He would say, "Sure, c'mon over." Always had time for us … a very nice guy.

I had heard from numerous accounts that Ford would pick on a certain actor throughout shooting. Did you witness any of this behavior?

I never witnessed this behavior. However, if he did, it was done on the quiet, probably when they would huddle together to discuss a scene.

Tell me about the other stars, like Jack Holt.

Jack Holt was another quiet guy. He really took his part very seriously. I say that because he was cast as a general in this picture and he had to look his best at all times and he was always walking around between takes smoking a cigarette and without a shirt because it was considered undignified for an officer to sweat. So, whenever they weren't filming a scene with Mr. Holt, he would take his shirt off and usually tie it around his waist until they were ready for the next shot because it was rather hot in that sun.

How about John Ford? How did he direct the picture? Was he loud? Did he bark orders at the actors and crew?

The only time I ever heard Ford talk loud or yell was during one scene that they were shooting where Jack Holt and Robert Montgomery were having a conversation by a jeep. Now, mind you, this was only a rehearsal. But, after they finished their discussion, the jeep took off and three stagehands threw some gravel and dirt under the tires of the jeep as it sped off, giving the illusion that the vehicle had "peeled out" hurriedly. When Ford saw that, he yelled at the top of his lungs, "Who the hell told you to do that?" I think everybody in the company heard him yelling.

Did you get to talk to John Ford?

Yes, the first day we were going out to the island for the shoot, I didn't know where I was supposed to go and I asked someone, who told me to just get on one of the boats. I jumped on the boat and John Ford was sitting aft and I happened to be sitting at his feet, not knowing who he was, but I knew he was somebody important.

As we were going out to the island, he began asking me some questions (I think he could see that I was very timid) like what my name was, where I was from, what I wanted to do with my life after my stint in the Navy. Pretty basic stuff.... When he heard that I was very interested in photography, he made it his business to introduce me to the MGM studio still photographer, Bert Lynch, who took me under his wing from then on. I couldn't get over the fact that this big Hollywood director really took an interest in me and our conversation lasted for about 20 minutes. After that, I had much respect for this man, whom I looked upon as a filmmaking genius.

Tell me about John Ford's "right-hand man," Jack Pennick.

Now, there's a guy who I can't say enough about. I don't know what he got paid, but whatever it was, it should have at least been double! He worked more than anyone on the set. He was always within five or six feet away of John Ford and whatever Ford wanted, Jack Pennick would oblige him immediately and efficiently. He was a "jack of all trades."

II. The Photographer

Tell me about Cameron Mitchell. I believe you knew him from our hometown of Stamford, Connecticut.

That's right! I met Cameron Mitchell in 1942 at the baseball field at Stamford High School. He was the sports announcer for our local radio station, WSRR, and he would be sitting out by the field during the games or practice and he would take notes during local sports events. He always had an entourage of people surrounding him and I would sit close by and listen to what he had to say. I was never formally introduced to him until we were both on the set of *They Were Expendable.* One day, when they were between shooting the picture, I happened to see this familiar face and I walked up to Jack Pennick and asked, "Who is that young fellow sitting over there?" and Jack responded, "Oh, some ham actor!" So, I walked over to Cameron and we talked a bit about Stamford and he was telling me how excited he was to be in this important Hollywood production working with John Ford.

How long did it take for the carpenters and crew to build the sets and what were the sets made of?

I never witnessed the construction of the sets. When I first arrived, the sets were already built, and all those buildings that you see were made out of bamboo, straw and wood. Incidentally, what the audience saw on screen was all you saw because there were no backs to any of the buildings. They were merely facades. If these fronts of the buildings had their doors open during shooting, they would put up a black curtain behind the door to conceal the fact that these weren't real buildings.

Were there any weather delays? If so, what did you do during these delays?

We had absolutely no delays. The weather was perfect. The only time we had a delay, and it didn't have to do with weather, was once when the boom man was given orders to stand by to do his audio work. All of a sudden, he would blow a whistle to stop everything while an overhead airplane was hovering over us. At first, nobody could hear the plane and Ford would ask, "What's the problem?" and the soundman would say, "Plane coming overhead."

How long would it take for a certain scene to be filmed?

As I said, all the sets were already built and set up before any of the actors got there and when they got there, they were ready to shoot. The cameras would be set up early in the morning and the cameramen would be consulting with John Ford about the various angles and lighting. I have a photograph in the collection with Ford working in very close proximity with the cameraman.

So, was it Ford who selected where the camera would be set up and not the cameraman?

Ford would usually look through the viewfinder and tell the cameraman what he wanted the shot to include and then the cameraman would make suggestions, but the final decision was Ford's. He was the "skipper" and he ran a tight ship.

What was Ford's technical crew like?

Very efficient. They knew exactly what the director wanted. John Ford very rarely had to tell them what to do. I suppose most of them had worked for Ford before and they were used to his methods of working.

You must tell me about Bert Lynch, the MGM studio still photographer.

Well, he was my best friend after Ford introduced me to him. I got to know him very well because of our mutual interests in photography. Since I was just a novice, he took me "under his wing" so to speak and he taught me an awful lot. Every time when he wasn't taking pictures, I would walk up to him and ask questions and he would patiently answer each and every one of them. In many of the photographs, you will see me talking to him. I would follow him around and make mental notes of everything he did and watch every step he would make when taking photographs. I can't say enough good things about Bert Lynch … very intelligent … very nice fellow. I still use many of the techniques he taught me up to this very day.

Did you keep in touch with Bert after the war?

No, I didn't keep in touch with anyone. I felt that this was going to be a "one time" thing and I was lucky to be there in the first place.

There are some photographs in the collection of you with Bert Lynch. Who took those pictures?

Remember when I told you that two of us had volunteered to be on the entire location shoot of *They Were Expendable* from the lab? That was Louis St. Pierre, who is in the photo sitting between John Wayne and Ward Bond.

II. The Photographer

What time of day did they usually finish shooting?
There was no specific time. Usually, it was between four and five o'clock.

Did they have a facility to view the "daily rushes?"
No, everything was shipped out to MGM.

What about the evenings after shooting? I've heard that John Ford, Wayne, Bond and the others used to love to indulge and party. Any reminiscences? Did you get to mingle with them?
No, I didn't get to mingle with them and I didn't know what they did after they finished shooting each day because I would jump off the PT boat at Miami shore to get back to the Sub Chaser Training Center.

What about visitors to the set?
There were a number of visitors including generals from the army and admirals from the navy and they would all congregate around John Ford, who would "light up" whenever they would come for a visit. You could see that Ford was elated by their presence on the set. Also, I was surprised to see that Richard Barthelmess came to the location for a visit. At the time, I didn't know who he was, but later I was to learn that he was a big star in silent movies. He and Robert Montgomery spent a lot of time together on the set.

Please tell me about Robert Barrat, who played General MacArthur in the movie. I had heard that everybody treated Barrat like he was actually General MacArthur. Is that true?
I think you hit it right on the head because I feel they intentionally wanted to create some kind of fake "aura" about him because everyone was so in awe of the real General MacArthur and it shows in the photograph I have of him sitting in a chair resting ... no one would go near him. Everybody stayed away from him and I was thinking that maybe he might be a relative of the real general or something (laughs).

Did you get to eavesdrop on anything interesting since you were situated so closely to all the action?
I did get to see John Wayne and Bob Montgomery clowning around a few times. I did take some photos of them fooling around and laughing.

Behind the Scenes of *They Were Expendable*

There was one particular time when Ward Bond and Montgomery were having a pretty heated discussion. I don't think the two of them got on that well during the filming. I felt that Montgomery would only speak to Bond if he absolutely had to.

Tell me about the last day of shooting.
On one particular day, I noticed that a ferry had come to pick up the entire cast and crew to take them away and that's how I knew that the filming had ended.

Was there a "wrap-up" party afterwards?
There was, but I wasn't invited. I had heard that it took place at the Plaza at Miami Beach and a big celebration with a parade took place and I remember John Wayne sitting in a big convertible and all the women were lined up in the streets waiting for his car to pass and they all began clamoring for him, kissing and touching him and he was all smiles, obviously enjoying every minute of it.

When did you first get to see* They Were Expendable?
I saw it in Miami ... I think it was in January of 1946.

What did you think of the movie?
I thought it was excellent! Not just because I was on the set but it was based on a true story and I read the book and the movie followed it pretty closely.

Any comments you'd like to make about the experience?
Yes, it was something that I will never forget, especially because I was in awe of John Wayne and Robert Montgomery through their movies. After all, these were real people who I never thought I would ever get to see in person, much less meet. Next to being married to my wonderful wife, Ann and having three wonderful sons, Jim, Paul and Steven, as well as my grandchildren, this was one of the highlights of my life.

When were you discharged from the Navy?
I was discharged from the Navy on June 6, 1946.

II. The Photographer

What are your plans now?

At my age, I try to tell myself to slow down, but it's very difficult. I guess I'm going to try to relax and enjoy my three grandchildren, Christopher, Michaela and Dominic, who are my life. My wife, Ann, passed away six years ago, but life goes on.

III: The Photographs

Female extra, who is shown in "close-up," crying, 21 minutes into *They Were Expendable* (pictured with her husband). Both were from the Philippines and had interpreters on the set.

Aftermath of the Philippines bombing. Sets were made of papier mâché, wood straw and bamboo. The telephone wires (pictured left) and the roof of barn with smoke stack (pictured center) were all matted out of the finished film. Note: This is the same area where the two extras in the preceding picture are standing.

III. The Photographs

Outdoor location set of torpedo boat squadron headquarters (note buildings in background three blocks away from Biscayne Boulevard and Flagler Street in Miami). "Prop debris" is scattered in the foreground for authenticity.

Behind the Scenes of *They Were Expendable*

Close-up of Motor Torpedo Squadron Headquarters set.

Opposite, top: Results of "bombing" with the American flag adding to the authenticity. Nick was justifiably proud of this shot.
Opposite, bottom: Mock-up carnage aftermath.

Shot of a real .50 caliber machine gun used in film.

III. The Photographs

Shot of PT boats showing the close proximity between the location shooting and the Miami shore, with actors and crew readying to board. Buildings were "matted" out of the film.

Opposite, bottom left: Robert Montgomery was always cooperative to strike a pose for servicemen and visitors. This shot was taken on the Miami shore. One of Nick's fondest recollections about Montgomery was when everybody was in line for mess waiting to get their boxed lunches. Nick related, "I let all of the actors, technicians, etc., get in line ahead of me and then I noticed Bob Montgomery standing behind me three back. I yelled to him to cut in front of me and he quickly told me, 'No, thanks! We're all equal here.'"

Opposite, bottom right: Ward Bond on a crutch in Miami, Florida (note building in background). Bond had been injured in an automobile accident prior to shooting and had a cast on his left foot. He used a regular crutch between scenes rather than the prop bamboo crutch used in the picture. Whenever they needed a shot of him walking, Ford had to use a stand-in and show him from behind.

Behind the Scenes of *They Were Expendable*

Shot of the PT boats docking at one of the small, uninhabited islands where most of the location shooting took place. Note the calmness of the water, as opposed to Key Biscayne, where the waters were much rougher and shooting would have been more difficult.

III. The Photographs

Nick asked John Wayne if he would pose for a picture. Wayne responded kiddingly, "Sure, if you'll give me a cigarette." Duke is holding the cigarette that Nick gave him.

Cameron Mitchell (right) sits with one of the "crew members" while awaiting instructions.

Behind the Scenes of *They Were Expendable*

Wayne and Cameron Mitchell having a friendly discussion. According to Nick, Cameron Mitchell lived in Stamford, Connecticut (Nick's hometown) at 138 Woodside Village off Summer Street. He also remembered a time when Mitchell was sitting behind Stamford High School with a bunch of friends watching the varsity baseball team practicing. Mitchell had been a radio announcer on WSRR, a local station in Stamford. When Nick saw him on the set and recognized him from his hometown, he asked Ford's "right-hand man" Jack Pennick who the young fellow was; he responded that he was some "ham actor."

Opposite: Shot of John Wayne and John Ford's assistant, Jack Pennick (in cap), wringing out a sweaty shirt while Bob Montgomery sits and chats with Ward Bond (recognizable by his injured foot). Ford's brother, assistant director Edward O'Fearna (with pipe in white shirt and tie), stands by.

III. The Photographs

Behind the Scenes of *They Were Expendable*

Montgomery attempting to bond with Bond.

III. The Photographs

Another shot of Robert Montgomery and Ward Bond relaxing between takes. In the background is the #34 boat with two extras on board going over the script.

"Duke" showing off his inimitable smile.

Behind the Scenes of *They Were Expendable*

Ford (under umbrella with camera) shooting a scene. Nick Scutti is the sailor in the foreground with rolled-up sleeves looking on. It was especially hot that day so the cast and crew would retreat to shady areas to get away from the blazing sun.

III. The Photographs

Directing an actual scene, with MGM studio still photographer Bert Lynch (extreme right) taking some publicity shots while Ford (seated behind camera) watches his cast at work.

III. The Photographs

Wayne translating for John Ford as he gives direction to the Filipino extra. Ford's brother and assistant director, Edward O'Fearna (with tie), stands by on the far left.

Opposite, top: Ford (center) talking over a scene with his cast while the continuity clerk (right) stands by with a script.
 Opposite, bottom: Nick Scutti (with back to camera and hands on hips in foreground) watching John Ford (far left) directing one of the Filipino extras. The extra needed translation, which was provided by John Wayne (holding rifle), who was fluent in Spanish.

III. The Photographs

Setting up the area for a set of "takes" with the scrim (a round silken device, which softens the harsh rays from the sun). Bob Montgomery walking into the scene with Ward Bond (with crutch) taking instructions from Pappy (pictured center with pipe). Boom microphone technician awaits further orders.

Opposite, top: Jack Pennick (on truck) loading small children and various furniture props onto a truck getting ready to leave the island while Duke looks on. "Pappy" Ford looks defiantly at the Filipino extra.

Opposite, bottom: Part-time assistant director Jack Pennick giving instructions to the boom (microphone) man, before he climbs the ladder. Ford sits next to the camera under the umbrella attempting to stay out of the sun.

Ward Bond (left) and Robert Montgomery involved in a rather heated conversation over their next scene. The two men did not get along.

After the scene is shot, principals Cameron Mitchell (foreground, in shorts) and Ward Bond stand by awaiting their next scene. Note Bond's prop crutch and a protective covering over his injured foot to protect the cast.

III. The Photographs

Actual shooting of Ward Bond being photographed on the Philippines set. Note MGM Studio still photographer Bert Lynch's 8 × 10 View Camera on tripod (to the left of the picture) used for taking publicity stills for the movie. They would later be exhibited in theater lobbies and theater glass cases to lure patrons inside. The young sailor in white, seated with his back to the camera, observing the proceedings, is Naval Lab photographer Bill Atwood.

Behind the Scenes of *They Were Expendable*

Studio still photographer Bert Lynch (kneeling center) taking shots with a 4 × 5 Speed Graphic. Actor Marshall Thompson (Ensign "Snake" Gardner) stands by on right, in cap. Jack Pennick (sans shirt) is on the left, and Bob Montgomery sits in the foreground awaiting the next scene.

Opposite: Ford (center with back to camera) confers with cameraman and his assistant before shooting a scene. Robert Montgomery waits patiently while a studio stagehand adds some shadowing with a palm fond for dramatic effect to an extreme close-up. Nick was situated behind Ford on a ladder when he took this fascinating photograph.

III. The Photographs

Behind the Scenes of *They Were Expendable*

Still photographer Bert Lynch aiming his 4 × 5 Speed Graphic, preparing to photograph a scene. Marshall Thompson (shirtless in sailor hat) stands by, on the left.

III. The Photographs

Bert Lynch (pictured center) is holding tote bag with additional film holders for his camera. Wayne and Ford (center in distance) are having a discussion. There is much waiting on a movie set while technicians set up their equipment.

The setting on one of the uncharted islands used for filming. It's definitely not Key Biscayne.

Opposite: Prop huts erected on an uncharted island used for filming.

III. The Photographs

Top, left: Pedro de Cordoba in character playing a priest. His entire role was deleted prior to the film's release. In later years, Ford had always claimed that character actor Wallace Ford donned the vestal garments. But, as this photograph proves, Ford's memory had failed him.

Top, right: One of the few actresses working on location, cast as a nun. Her part also ended up on the cutting room floor.

Another shot of de Cordoba as the priest standing in front of the studio-built chapel (the sequence was shot but later jettisoned from the finished picture).

III. The Photographs

Pedro de Cordoba and three "nun" extras in another scene not used in the finished picture.

Behind the Scenes of *They Were Expendable*

Navy lab photographer Bill Atwood (Nick's buddy) enters the mock chapel, which wasn't used in the final cut.

Another shot of the chapel with John Wayne and Robert Montgomery talking to the priest (Pedro de Cordoba). The scene was later discarded.

Wayne in a typical pose with trademark smile and hands on hips, happily obliging Nick Scutti with another photograph.

Navy WAVES invited to the set are thrilled to meet Robert Montgomery. Montgomery was always gracious to any visitor who happened by.

John Ford talks to two Naval officer nurses visiting the location. Ford was always very kind to everyone from the Armed Forces who happened by.

Lieutenant Brickley's PT boat #41. Note the seaman readying to throw a line to dock the vessel.

Behind the Scenes of *They Were Expendable*

Brickley vessel coming to dock. Notice the tattered American flag, twin .50 caliber machine gun on deck and fake torpedo on the right and left. Each boat had four torpedo tubes.

III. The Photographs

Another vessel coming in to dock with its aft torpedo tube figuring prominently in the photograph. Another boat (distant center) follows to dock.

Behind the Scenes of *They Were Expendable*

Rusty's #32 boat.

Shot of the stern of one of the PT boats used in the film with the camera crew (under umbrella) and scrim (a device used to soften the appearance of a character's face in close-up) getting ready for a shot. A scrim was used most notably in the scene at the Officer's Ball where Donna Reed asks Rusty (Wayne) if he cares to dance. The close-up shot of Reed is photographed in soft focus using this device to conceal her freckles.

After the shooting of a scene, Jack Holt removes his shirt during the break, not only to cool off and catch some rays, but also not to perspire through his uniform. The wardrobe department and director Ford would never allow any signs of perspiration on the uniforms of any actors portraying top-ranking officers. A studio technician (far right) rests the boom microphone pole, which carries the wiring for the sound to the generator.

Jack Holt relaxing and enjoying a smoke during the break. Nick revealed that Holt was always smoking when not in front of the camera. He also described him as a friendly guy who was open to conversation.

Holt posing with one of Nick's fellow lab buddies, Norm Shaver.

Jack Holt's famous profile.

Actual scene being taken of General Martin (Jack Holt) with bodyguard extra.

III. The Photographs

Shooting scene of Jack Holt with "bodyguards," as boom mike technician stands on an overturned rowboat to get the proper height. Note assistant Jack Pennick in foreground making sure he's not in the scene. Pennick would follow Ford around constantly during the shoot and knew exactly what Ford wanted and got it right. If Ford needed anything, Pennick readily obliged!

Behind the Scenes of *They Were Expendable*

Nick's pal Louis St. Pierre photographs Nick (center) as he sits with John Wayne (left) and Ward Bond during lunch break.

III. The Photographs

Now, it was Nick's turn to take a shot of Louis St. Pierre seated between Wayne and Bond during the lunch break. Before this photograph was taken, Nick asked Ward Bond if it would be okay for him to take the picture. Bond's remarks were NOT pleasant to hear (note his body language) and he told Nick, "Leave us alone!" Wayne interceded and, admonishing Bond, said, "Ah, let 'em take the picture!"

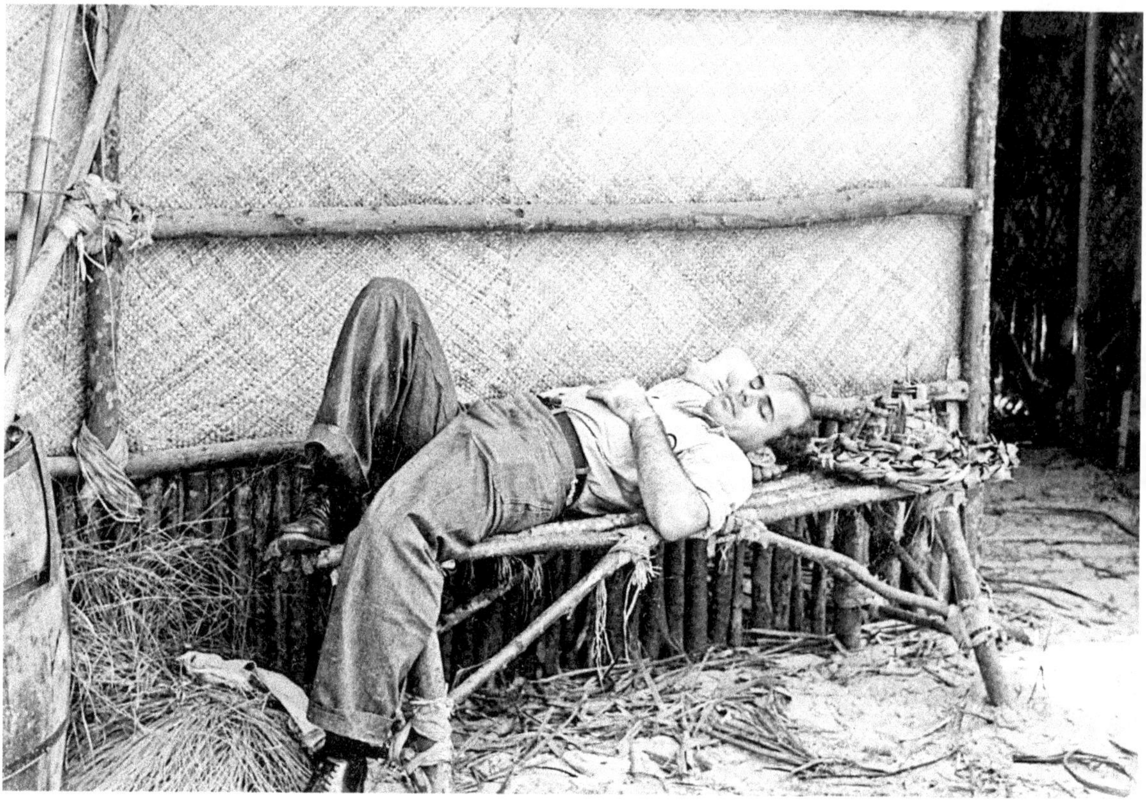

III. The Photographs

John Wayne, Jack Holt and (with back to camera) Robert Montgomery in a photograph taken during the shooting of a scene.

Opposite, top: After lunch, Nick pretends to take forty winks in front of a façade of a bamboo hut. Inside Nick's shirt pocket is a twelve-exposure film pack that he used instead of using a film holder, which only held two exposures. He had to keep well supplied because he was there during all of the location shooting, which took a month. Nick was 18 years old in 1945, when the picture was filmed.
  Opposite, bottom: Louie St. Pierre is taking a nap as well.

III. The Photographs

Ford (note the officer's insignia on his hat) directing a scene with the principals. To the rear of the jeep is the man in charge of continuity.

Opposite, top: Similar scene with John Ford (right) discussing the shot with principals Wayne, Montgomery, Holt and Charles Trowbridge (Admiral Blackwell; seated in a jeep). Charles Trowbridge was described as very amiable and quiet.

Opposite, bottom: Different angle of Charles Trowbridge (sitting in jeep on passenger side) with Jack Holt in the back seat. Ford (in baseball cap above windshield) could be seen in the background. Jack Pennick sits on the hood.

III. The Photographs

Another shot of "Pappy" Ford discussing a scene with Holt, Montgomery and Wayne. Note the boom microphone (wrapped in material to cut down on any intrusive noises) and the sound technician (far right on ladder) waiting for the scene to begin. Just before this particular scene was shot, the technician delayed shooting due to airplanes flying overhead.

Opposite, top: Montgomery and Wayne conferring with Charles Trowbridge as Ford stands by in background.
Opposite, bottom: Charles Trowbridge as he's getting ready to leave the area after the scene was shot.

Behind the Scenes of *They Were Expendable*

Getting ready for another scene with Jack Pennick (shirtless), Wayne and Montgomery (looking down) and Ford, with his back to the camera, positioning the shot.

Opposite, top: Actual shooting of a scene of Montgomery and Wayne asking Jack Holt if there was any information from headquarters requesting the usage of their PT boats. Note the boom microphone and reflector in close proximity.
  Opposite, bottom: After being admonished by John Wayne the previous day for not wanting Nick to photograph him, Ward Bond, during a break, called to Nick and asked him if he still wanted to take his picture. The result: Bond hamming it up for the camera and holding his gut in. One of Nick's buddies took this shot.

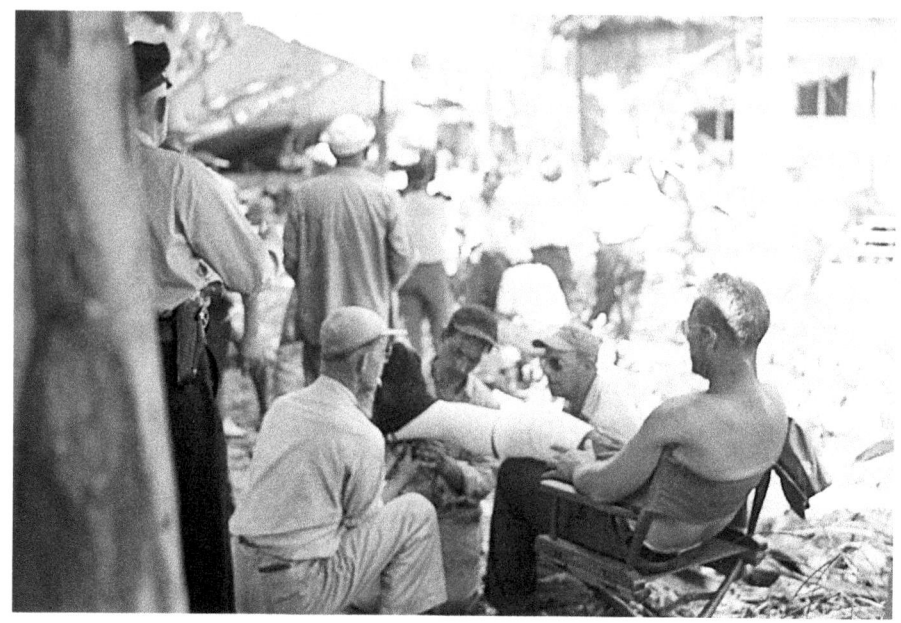

Doctors tending to Ward Bond's injury and applying a "protective" stocking over his right foot to keep the cast clean.

Robert Montgomery and Ward Bond crossing the studio-built bridge, with extras carrying the "wounded."

III. The Photographs

Montgomery, Bond and "crew members" marching across the bridge after the bombing of their headquarters.

Behind the Scenes of *They Were Expendable*

Establishing shot of the same scene with bullet-ridden panel truck in the water in the foreground.

III. The Photographs

Different angle of "crew" marching across the bridge.

Shot of the same scene showing bullet-riddled truck. The bullet holes, simulating gunfire from an aircraft, were put there by a prop man.

Studio stagehand making smoke with torch to enact the aftermath of the bombing. Moments later, this same man was bitten by a snake and was taken away by boat to a nearby hospital in Miami. Nobody ever knew what happened to him.

III. The Photographs

Cameron Mitchell (top left) poses with members of the "crew." Alex Havier, who played Benny Lecoco, is on the bottom right.

III. The Photographs

Actual shooting of the scene.

Opposite, top: Some clowning with a pair of binoculars from the principals while Jack Holt (left, sans shirt) looks totally uninterested.

Opposite, bottom: Right before the actual shooting of one of the last scenes of the picture with Ward Bond (with crutch) and the "survivors" getting ready to aid the army "wherever the army can use you." A young Marshall Thompson is on the left (with a gun).

Behind the Scenes of *They Were Expendable*

Rehearsing a scene with Montgomery and Marshall Thompson (right). Ward Bond seems to be interested in something off camera.

Opposite, top: As we pan back from the last photograph, we see camera crew and assistant cameraman framing a shot while still photographer Bert Lynch is ready with his 8 × 10 view camera to snap some publicity stills. The bag hanging off the tripod contains 8 × 10 film holders. Ford's chair is to the left of the 35mm camera and a boom rod is seen leaning against a ladder.

Opposite, bottom: One of the final scenes shot on location, with Bob Montgomery and Duke saying good-bye to Ward Bond and various "survivors." A cloth-laden boom is being held by the sound technician pictured on the right, with continuity man John Banse standing by, with arms crossed.

Ward Bond (with prop crutch) receives binoculars from Robert Montgomery after he tells him to take charge in a scene from the film. John Wayne (barely visible) looks on.

Actual location when the remaining crew members are about to embark on a plane to join forces with the Army on orders from Commanding Officer Brickley (Robert Montgomery).

III. The Photographs

Nick Scutti and Robert Montgomery. Nick said that Montgomery used to like to occasionally have his lunch secluded from the rest of the cast and crew. On this particular day, Nick happened by with a buddy of his (who took this picture) and asked him if he wouldn't mind posing with him for another shot. Montgomery gladly obliged and invited them both to join him for lunch.

III. The Photographs

Location sets with extras waiting for instructions.

Opposite, top: Extras milling around waiting patiently for the next scene. Waiting seemed endless on a movie set.
Opposite, bottom: More studio-built sets, including the cantina.

Behind the Scenes of *They Were Expendable*

Closer shot of the cantina, with extras walking around or sitting between takes.

Opposite, top: Shooting a scene with Jack Holt. It's a wonder that actors could concentrate with so much activity going on while the cameras were rolling.

Opposite, bottom: Bill Atwood, naval photographer and Nick's buddy, peruses the set.

Ward Bond getting ready for another "take" with his prop bamboo crutch, in a shot that can be seen in the film.

III. The Photographs

Ward Bond's double waiting to be called for a scene.

Ward Bond's double (in hat) with the make-up man as he's putting final touches on one of the extras.

Nick posing in front of a mock hut set.

III. The Photographs

Robert Barrat as General Douglas MacArthur sits patiently waiting to film a scene. The boom man in the background (on ladder) getting ready.

III. The Photographs

Actual shooting of MacArthur (Robert Barrat) leaving PT boat, Jack Holt saluting and Ward Bond looking on.

Opposite, top: Jack Pennick (shirtless, center right) conferring with the continuity man before shooting a scene, as Bob Montgomery and Ward Bond share a laugh.
   Opposite, bottom: Preparing to shoot the scene with General MacArthur disembarking from boat #41, as the cast and ample crew and technicians go about their business.

Behind the Scenes of *They Were Expendable*

Medium shot of General MacArthur (Robert Barrat) extending his hand to Jack Holt as he leaves the boat, taken during actual shoot. Bob Montgomery salutes as Ward Bond (on far right, not seen in finished film) observes.

Opposite, top: MacArthur (Robert Barrat) thanks Jack Holt and Charles Trowbridge for assisting him in his effort to get to Australia (in an actual scene from film).

Opposite, bottom: Photograph of John Ford (on ground) discussing next scene to be filmed with actors Robert Montgomery, Jack Holt and John Wayne (left to right). Nick stated that this conference took about 10 minutes and the three actors listened intently while Ford gave directions. During the shooting, the three principals were supposed to ride off quickly in a jeep. Out of camera range, there were three studio stagehands, who thought they were supposed to throw dirt and sand underneath the rear tires of the jeep to simulate clouds of dust as the jeep departed. To the dismay of the stagehands, Ford never asked for that particular effect, and loudly and harshly admonished the three men for not consulting with him first.

More intense discussion.

Jack Holt, "Duke" Wayne and Bob Montgomery posing for another photograph.

III. The Photographs

Between scenes, it was a common occurrence to see Bob Montgomery zipping around on a borrowed motorcycle. Barely visible on the side of the station wagon is the name Key Biscayne. Could it be that this vehicle was used for publicity purposes?

III. The Photographs

Duke posing with a grip between takes.

Opposite, top: Montgomery involved in some casual conversation with extras between takes.
　Opposite, bottom: Robert Montgomery (sitting in jeep) with John Ford going over a scene with character actor Russell Simpson (center). John Wayne looks in (far right, foreground).

Behind the Scenes of *They Were Expendable*

John Wayne posing with another member of the Naval Photo Lab, Chester Pence.

Character actor Murray Alper ("Slug" Mahan) with an extra obligingly hamming it up for Nick.

Left: Close-up of Murray Alper. Nick said Murray was lots of fun to be around and would obligingly pose for snapshots for the numerous visitors to the set.

Right: Montgomery (left) and Wayne barely able to strike a serious pose after some tomfoolery on the set.

Montgomery (left) and Wayne clowning around for the camera.

Studio lights that were used for some interior shots, reflectors, and other assorted equipment for shooting on location.

MGM studio still photographer Bert Lynch, caught off guard, standing next to his 8 × 10 View Camera. Ward Bond sits relaxing nearby, with his prop bamboo crutch.

III. The Photographs

Nick (pictured left) getting some pointers from MGM still cameraman Bert Lynch. Bert patiently answered all of his questions about photography and to this day Nick uses many of the techniques he learned from him.

Behind the Scenes of *They Were Expendable*

III. The Photographs

John Ford (center with pipe) along with some two- and three-star admirals and other high-ranking naval officers clamoring around Commander Richard Barthelmess during the latter's visit to the set. The only cast member present is Robert Montgomery (center, with back to camera).

Opposite, top: A surprise visitor: Silent film great Richard Barthelmess (left), now a lieutenant commander, visits the set, to the delight of Robert Montgomery.
  Opposite, bottom: Robert Montgomery having a conversation with a vice-admiral who was visiting the set, while Richard Barthelmess listens.

III. The Photographs

Pappy standing center stage overlooking camera set-up while Bert Lynch talks with the continuity clerk (seated), inquiring about the next scene. A sound man (on ladder) checks for sound quality. Wayne stands behind Bert Lynch.

Opposite, top: A three-star admiral and two-star general and bodyguards as guests on the set with Ford and Montgomery enjoying their visit with Richard Barthelmess. John Wayne is curiously absent: Ford wouldn't allow Wayne to mingle with high-ranking officers.

Opposite, bottom: Bob Montgomery waiting for his cue for the next scene as he stands in front of a PT boat.

Behind the Scenes of *They Were Expendable*

Wayne (third from left with back to camera) keeps his distance from naval dignitaries and visitor Richard Barthelmess, who's conversing with Bob Montgomery (in shorts with back to camera). Ford stands in front of Montgomery in a black baseball cap. In the foreground (center right) is Joe Maddock, who was the head of the Naval Photographic Lab.

III. The Photographs

Cameron Mitchell, John Wayne, Robert Montgomery, Ward Bond and "crew" rehearsing a scene at the back of a boat. Some of the remaining crew members await orders to leave their unit.

III. The Photographs

A side view of the PT boat being pulled up from the water.

Opposite, top: Wayne (left) watching the extras taking the shim away from the base of the vessel getting ready to tow Montgomery's 41 boat. Note the stains on the boat near the exhaust pipes. These were applied by a studio technician to give the effect of realism.
Opposite, bottom: A side view of the PT boat on land.

III. The Photographs

John Ford was adamant that no shots of the starboard side of the PT boat were to be photographed, which would reveal the fact that the boat was a mock-up made of wood with struts holding up the side. During a lunch break, while no one was near the set, Nick took his camera and snuck around the boat and discreetly snapped a picture so he could show his friends and family back home how movies were made. Note the wheels underneath the "boat" used for towing (see previous photograph). Also, the stains weren't yet added to the exhaust pipes.

Opposite, top: Assistant Jack Pennick (to left on ladder), getting the boat ready for the next scene, is about to accept a saw from a studio hand for some minor alterations on the boat. The sound man on ladder holding boom microphone is waiting for instructions from Pennick. Studio carpenters were kept busy on the set before cameras began to roll.

Opposite, bottom: Shot of tractor (on left) towing a PT boat. Note the simulated damage on the boat from enemy gun fire.

Behind the Scenes of *They Were Expendable*

Shot of rear skeleton of a studio-built dwelling (in the background) with a truck getting ready to tow the PT boat. The men in white shirts and ties are firemen visiting the set.

III. The Photographs

Shot of a fishing boat and prop hut used in the film.

Top: A PT boat (in distance) leaves the dock, with a scenic view of the bamboo hut on the right.

Bottom: PT boats and boat on right carrying extras going out to one of the small uncharted islands taken from the bow of one of the PT boats. On one of the boats from Miami to one of the small islands John Ford came up to Nick and talked with him throughout the 20-minute ride, asking him where he was from, what he intended to do after he got out of the Navy, what his interests were. He took a genuine interest in many of the young sailors who happened to be on the set. On other occasions, the actors used to drive the PT boats, fooling around and racing as they returned to their home port.

IV. The Real Heroes

Rear Admiral John D. Bulkeley, USN (1911–1996)

Born in New York on August 9, 1911, John D. Bulkeley spent most of his childhood in Marblehead, Massachusetts, a coastal town along the Atlantic Ocean in Essex County. During his teens, his family relocated to Hackettstown, New Jersey, where he graduated from high school in 1928. A year later, he entered the U.S. Navy Academy, graduating on June 1, 1933. Following that, he was a commissioned ensign and on May 29, 1937, he was promoted to lieutenant (j.g.) after serving aboard the USS *Indianapolis*, USS *Chaumont*, USS *Sacramento* and USS *Saratoga*. Later, he commanded Submarine Chaser Division Two in February and March of 1941 and on April 1, 1941, he was once again promoted to lieutenant commander, where for five months, he served as commander of Submarine Chaser Division One. In August later that year, he was given command of the Motor Torpedo Boat Squadron Three. It was this squadron's actions in the Philippine campaign that were so accurately depicted in *They Were Expendable.* Three days after the attack on the Cavite Navy Yard in Pearl Harbor, on that fateful day of December 7, 1941, Bulkeley's squadron retaliated against the Japanese. He was decorated for "meritorious service" following this.

His biggest triumph came shortly after when he broke through Japanese lines at Corregidor and Bataan, where he was ordered to transport Gen. Douglas MacArthur and his staff, along with their families, to safety on Mindanao Island, after which MacArthur was shipped off to Australia to command the Armed Forces in the Pacific. This historic episode is also depicted accurately in *They Were Expendable.*

Behind the Scenes of *They Were Expendable*

After this, Bulkeley was sent to the Negros Island where he broke through the Japanese lines and transported Philippine President Manuel L. Quezon (1878–1944), his staff and their families to Mindanao, where they were also to be flown to Australia to safety. Quezon, who was the first president to be elected through a national election of the Commonwealth of the Philippines from 1935 to 1944, was responsible for sympathizing with the landless peasants as well as reorganizing the island's military defense and fought against graft and corruption within his government. Later, he was sent to the United States where he served the Commonwealth government in exile with headquarters in Washington, D.C.

John D. Bulkeley was then ordered to stay behind in the Philippines holding guerrilla maneuvers while under attack until orders were sent from Gen. MacArthur to stop all military action after the collapse of the Japanese empire.

After the war, he was ordered to New Guinea where he participated in the battle of the Bismarck Sea, the invasion of Finschhafen and the Troborland Islands. For his heroic defense of the Philippines, now Commander Bulkeley was awarded the Medal of Honor ("For extraordinary heroism, distinguished service and conspicuous gallantry above and beyond the call of duty, as Commander of Motor Torpedo Boat Squadron Three in Philippine waters during the period December 7, 1941, to April 10, 1942"), the Navy Cross ("For extraordinary heroism as Commanding Officer of Motor Torpedo Boat Number 34 in connection with military operations against the Japanese enemy forces in the Philippine area"), the Army Distinguished Service Cross, the Army Silver Star Medal, the Army Distinguished Unit Badge and the Republic of the Philippines Distinguished Conduct Star (all for bravery). He was also a Purple Heart recipient after being wounded when the Japanese attacked in Marivelles Harbor, Bataan and the Philippine Islands on December 26, 1941. Pres. Charles DeGaulle of France presented him with the Croix de Guerre for his part in the Invasion of Normandy.

His postwar duties had him assuming command of the USS *Stribling* on September 29, 1945, and a year later, was assigned to the staff of the Naval Academy and he remained there until May of 1948. Then, he was made executive officer on the USS *Mount Olympus*. Later, he attended school at the Armed Forces Staff College in Norfolk, Virginia, where he eventually became Chief of the Weapons Division of the Military Liaison Committee to

IV. The Real Heroes

the Atomic Energy Commission in the Office of the Secretary of Defense, researching and developing atomic weapons.

As the 1950s progressed, he was Staff Officer of the Joint Staff, Joint Chiefs of Staff from January 1956 to March of 1958 in Washington, D.C., Pres. John F. Kennedy approved of his selection for the rank of rear admiral on May 31, 1963, and he was awarded that title on February 1, 1964, after Kennedy's assassination. In the mid-sixties, he was commander of the Naval Base at Guantanamo Bay, Cuba, until June of 1966. Exactly a year later, he was back in Washington D.C., again serving as president of the Board of Inspection and Survey. He retired on New Years Day of 1974 and passed away on April 6, 1996.

Of his work with John Ford, he stated in a 1987 interview, "John Ford was a born leader, and he *used* it. Men followed him *willingly*."

Commander Robert B. Kelly, USN (1913–1989)

Born on June 9, 1913, in New York City, Robert B. Kelly graduated from the U.S. Naval Academy in Annapolis in 1935. During World War II, he was a PT boat lieutenant and second in command under Lt. John D. Bulkeley in the Motor Torpedo Boat Squadron Three. His heroic feats were based in part in the MGM wartime classic *They Were Expendable*, with John Wayne portraying him as Lt. (j.g.) "Rusty" Ryan.

Along with Lt. Bulkeley, Kelly was responsible for evacuating Gen. Douglas MacArthur from Corregidor, where the Japanese had American forces surrounded. His boat, PT-34, sank the Japanese cruiser *Kuma* and a Japanese torpedo boat, *Kiji*, in the Philippines off Cebu Island on April 8, 1942, events depicted in the movie. As a result, Kelly won the Silver Star for gallantry. The following day, his boat was attacked by Japanese bombers and four Japanese F1M flatboats near Kanuit Island, but he managed to dock the boat and get four of his six-man crew to ground safely. One man was killed in action and another drowned. Kelly was awarded the Navy Cross and was commended for "distinguished conduct and extraordinary courage in combat" and "despite extremely heavy shellfire, opposition and the fact that the cruiser was screened by four enemy destroyers, the PT-34 closed to 300 yard range and made two successful torpedo hits on the enemy cruiser,

Behind the Scenes of *They Were Expendable*

finally sinking her." This episode was also vividly depicted in *They Were Expendable*.

Later, Kelly would win the Silver Star as commander of a squadron of PT boats, which included the famed PT-109, the same boat that was destroyed and sunk under the command of Lt. John F. Kennedy. In 1945, now Lieutenant Commander Kelly was part of the invasion of Okinawa, and was awarded a Bronze Star.

After the war, Lt. Comm. Robert B. Kelly was in command of the ice breaker *Atka* between 1950 and 1956 and then on the destroyer *Shenandoah* in 1958–59. He was elevated to the rank of captain when he retired in 1961. He passed away on January 23, 1989, and had a son, Capt. Robert B. Kelly, Jr., who followed in his father's footsteps.

V. THE CELLULOID HEROES AND SUPPORTING CAST

Robert Montgomery (1904–1981)

Born Henry Montgomery, Jr., on May 21, 1904 (some sources say 1908) in Beacon, New York, Robert Montgomery, whose father was the president of a rubber company, had a very privileged childhood, where he was sent to exclusive private schools until his father's death in 1920. Due to poor investments, his family was left penniless and Robert was forced to work as a railroad mechanic and later as an oil tanker deckhand when he was in his late teens.

Moving to New York City, the young man decided to try his hand at writing short stories, which came to nothing. A friend of his liked his confident manner and good looks and persuaded him to try acting. His stage debut came in 1924 and at the end of the decade, he was a "featured attraction" on the Broadway stage. By 1929, he, along with some other fellow stage actors, ventured west to try to land work in the movies. This was a time when the new "talkie revolution" had caught Hollywood by storm and Bob found no trouble adapting to the new medium, due to the fact that he had been on the live stage and was already an old hand at distinctly delivering his lines. Once he arrived, he was immediately swept up by MGM, who had been looking for new talent from the stage in order to save money on speech classes from their roster of silent screen stars, many of whom were out of jobs once sound films became a reality.

After appearing in a few bit roles, one of Bob's earliest leading man roles came in silent comedian Buster Keaton's first talkie, *Free and Easy* (1930). Sadly, this seemed to be Montgomery's destiny for the time being, and he would be saddled with uninteresting stories with roles constantly typecasting him as the genial "boy next door," playing second fiddle to MGM's roster of female stars like Greta Garbo, Norma Shearer, Joan Crawford and Myrna Loy. Of course, some of the films, like *The Divorcee* (1930) and *Privates Lives* (1931) were quite good (the latter displaying Montgomery's innate charm and knack for comedy), but as a whole, his output, up to this time, was rather uninteresting.

In 1930, he won a substantial role in the 1930 prison epic *The Big House*, which was directed by George Hill, where he played a cowardly inmate opposite stars Chester Morris and Wallace Beery. The role didn't do much for his career (although he is quite good in it) and he soon found himself back again typecast as debonair leading men, usually attired in tuxedo and top hat.

Constantly fighting studio boss, Louis B. Mayer, for better assignments, he found, to his dismay, that his pleas were rudely ignored. In the mid-thirties, while vacationing in New York, Bob and his wife decided to take in a play called *Night Must Fall*, which starred Emlyn Williams, who also wrote it. Montgomery was so impressed by the stage production that when he returned to his studio, he pleaded that MGM buy the screen rights to the property.

The play, which was a very dark story about a psychopathic murderer who decapitates his female victims, came under close scrutiny by Louis B. Mayer, who felt that this was not the type of film fare MGM was known for producing, publicly denounced the movie and, as a result, had all prints withdrawn shortly after its release. *Night Must Fall* won rave reviews among critics, with Bland Johaneson of the *New York Daily Mirror* saying that it "represents a provocative imagination, a skilled adapter, a sensitive director, a splendid acting job." Other critics singled out Montgomery's performance as the "best of the year," while MGM tried valiantly to sweep the film "under the carpet," hoping to squash Montgomery's chances of capitalizing on the Oscar nomination he received. Studio heads rallied instead for Spencer Tracy's portrayal of the fatherly Portuguese fisherman, Manuel Fidello, in *Captains Courageous*. Tracy did win the Best Actor Academy Award of 1937.

To further irritate L.B. Mayer, in 1935, Robert Montgomery was elected president of the Screen Actors Guild (SAG), where he complained about poor labor conditions and long working hours among actors in Hollywood. Serving four terms, he would later gain much publicity when he exposed labor racketeering in the film industry.

Still fighting his studio bosses "tooth and nail" for some better film roles, he was able to land some rather interesting ones during this period, including *The Earl of Chicago, Busman's Holiday* (both 1940), as well as *Mr. and Mrs. Smith* (directed by Alfred Hitchcock) and the classic romantic comedy/fantasy *Here Comes Mr. Jordan* (both 1941).

Just prior to America's involvement in World War II, Robert Montgomery was commissioned a lieutenant in the U.S. Naval Reserve and served briefly as assistant naval attaché at the embassy in London and later lived in the White House, setting up naval operations overseas. He commanded a P.T. boat in the Pacific and was an operations officer aboard a destroyer during the invasion of France (D-Day). As a lieutenant commander, he was awarded the Bronze Star and was later decorated as a chevalier of the French Legion of Honor. Upon his discharge from the service, he returned to Hollywood to make *They Were Expendable* for MGM. It was during this filming that, late in production, director John Ford had an accident on the set and Robert Montgomery was personally asked by Ford, to finish directing the picture. Relishing this experience, he turned to directing his own vehicles, including *Lady in the Lady* (1946), a rather contrived but nevertheless interesting film noir effort, which was based on a Raymond Chandler murder mystery, told in the "first person" with Montgomery seen only briefly as he steps in front of mirrors. His next film was an improvement called *Ride the Pink Horse* (1947), another noir entry for Universal-International.

Like *They Were Expendable* co-star, John Wayne, Montgomery was a staunch conservative Republican and he later testified as a friendly witness during the opening sessions of the House of Un-American Activities Committee (HUAC) denouncing Communist infiltration in the movie industry. In 1952, he was appointed a special consultant to Pres. Dwight D. Eisenhower on public communications. In the early fifties, Robert Montgomery was back producing, directing and starring, not in movies, but for television in a classic, top-rated "anthology" series called *Robert Montgomery Presents*. In 1955, he returned to the Broadway stage as director of *The Desperate Hours*, for which he won a Tony as Best Director. In 1960, he directed his final film, *The Gallant Hours,* which he co-produced with the film's star, James Cagney.

His daughter, Elizabeth Montgomery, followed in her father's footsteps and became a popular television star in her own right in the popular hit series *Bewitched* in the 1960s. After a very full life in films, television, and in the Naval Reserve, where he was decorated numerous times, Robert

Behind the Scenes of *They Were Expendable*

Montgomery died on September 27, 1981. His accomplishments both in front of and behind the camera, as well as his heroic feats during World War II, are a credit to this extraordinary American.

Robert Montgomery films directed by John Ford:
They Were Expendable (1945)

John Wayne (1907–1979)

Born on May 26, 1907, in Winterest, Iowa, as Marion Robert Morrison, he later attended the University of Southern California (USC) on a football scholarship. After working at various jobs during his summer vacation with fellow football teammate and best friend, Ward Bond, both young men gained employment at the Fox Film Corporation as prop men for director John Ford. Ford immediately took a liking to the lanky (6'4½"), good-natured "Duke" Wayne (as he was known by this time) and gave him some bit roles in films like *Hangman's House* (1928) because of his good looks.

In 1930, Wayne received his first major role in Raoul Walsh's grand scale, big-budget western epic, *The Big Trail*, which was filmed in the experimental 65mm wide-screen process. Unfortunately, the film bombed at the box office and Wayne found himself in an almost seemingly endless run of "B" westerns for the most part. He was able to land small, minor roles in some major pictures like *The Life of Jimmy Dolan* and *Baby Face* (1933), but these films did absolutely nothing to advance his career. Besides doing supporting roles in Buck Jones and Tim McCoy westerns, Wayne was in approximately 80 low budget westerns, even cast as "Sandy" the singing cowboy for a short time, with his singing obviously dubbed. After laboring in these "quickies" for nine years, director John Ford convinced independent producer Walter Wanger to make a western based on the story *Stage to Lordsburg* by Ernest Haycox. Wanger had insisted on casting Gary Cooper for the lead role of the Ringo Kid, but Ford was adamant and wanted to use his protégé, John Wayne. Ford won out and *Stagecoach* was a tremendous hit and was nominated for six Academy Awards, including Best Picture. As a result, John Wayne was on the road to super-stardom.

Throughout the 1940s, Wayne was under a "non-exclusive" deal with "B" studio, Republic Pictures, and studio head, Hal Yates, did not want to lose his company's greatest commodity when the United States declared war on Japan after the attack on Pearl Harbor. In between filming westerns and adventure films for his home studio, Wayne found himself in great demand with the big studios and was cast in some very prestigious productions like John Ford's *The Long Voyage Home* (1940), based on several short stories by Eugene O'Neill, *The Shepherd of the Hills* (1941), which was Wayne's first Technicolor production and *Reap the Wild Wind* (1942), another Technicolor epic directed by Cecil B. DeMille. He also made three films for Universal with Marlene Dietrich as his co-star (*Seven Sinners*, *The Spoilers* and *Pittsburgh*).

When World War II broke out, Wayne tried to enlist, and there are many varying accounts as to why he never was in the military. One of these (and probably the most logical) was that Republic studio head, Herbert Yates, convinced government officials that Wayne would be more useful working in Hollywood making pro–American films rather than fighting overseas. Yates obviously did not want to lose his "golden goose." What resulted were some great "flag-wavers" including *The Fighting Seabees*, *Back to Bataan* and *They Were Expendable*.

Off screen, John Wayne was the personification of the conservative American, hell bent on preserving true American ideals and very vocal about it. During the McCarthy era, he co-founded the Motion Picture Alliance for the Preservation of American Ideals.

Following World War II, he made a string of box office hits, including *Fort Apache*, *Red River* (both 1948), *Three Godfathers*, *She Wore a Yellow Ribbon*, *Sands of Iwo Jima* (all 1949) and *Rio Grande* (1950). During this period, and throughout most of his film career, after becoming a major attraction, John Wayne was one of the top money-making stars at the box office in the movie industry and his string of continued successes included *The Quiet Man* (1952), *Island in the Sky*, *Hondo* (both 1953), *The High and the Mighty* (1954), *The Searchers* (1956), arguably the greatest western ever made, and *Rio Bravo* (1959).

After surviving lung cancer in the early sixties, Wayne's untiring drive still kept him in the ranks of the Hollywood elite throughout the decade with films like *The Man Who Shot Liberty Valance*, *How the West Was Won* (both 1962), *McLintock!* (1963) and *El Dorado* (1967). In 1969, he would win his only Academy Award as Rooster Cogburn in *True Grit*, which almost seemed like a consolation prize in light of his excellent previous works, which far outshined this later performance. As the next decade approached, he was still a top-ranked movie star despite his age (he was well into his sixties) and continued his successful winning streak of hits with *Rio Lobo* (1970), *The Cowboys* (1972) and *Brannigan* (1975).

Wayne's last movie would be *The Shootist* (1976), a rather poignant tale of an aging gunfighter, who is dying of cancer. Sadly, the movie almost seemed autobiographical because John Wayne was dying of stomach cancer. His last public appearance was at the 1979 Academy of Motion Pictures Arts and Sciences ceremony. Looking wane and underweight, he nevertheless showed true courage by appearing on the telecast. He died a few months later on June 11, 1979. A Congressional Medal of Honor was posthumously dedicated in his honor.

John Wayne films directed by John Ford:

Mother Machcree (1928)
Hangman's House (1928)
Four Sons (1928)
The Black Watch (1929)
Stagecoach (1939)
The Long Voyage Home (1940)
They Were Expendable (1945)
Fort Apache (1948)
Three Godfathers (1949)
She Wore a Yellow Ribbon (1949)
Rio Grande (1950)
The Quiet Man (1952)
The Searchers (1956)
The Wings of Eagles (1957)
The Horse Soldiers (1959)
The Man Who Shot Liberty Valance (1962)
How the West Was Won (1962)
Donovan's Reef (1963)

Donna Reed (1921–1986)

Born Donna Belle Mullenger on January 27, 1921, in Denison, Iowa, Donna Reed was brought up on her parents' farm. It was while attending Los Angeles City College that she decided to take up acting after winning the Campus Queen Beauty Contest. A talent scout from Metro-Goldwyn-Mayer saw her in an amateur stage production and she was signed to a contract in 1941. Billed as Donna Adams in her first movie, *The Get-Away*, and then as Donna Reed in her second venture, *Shadow of the Thin Man*, she was able to obtain more substantial roles in films like *The Courtship of Andy Hardy* and *Calling Dr. Gillespie.* She later received a rather sizable role in the prestigious William Saroyan adaptation of *The Human Comedy* (1943), starring Mickey Rooney. Donna was also seen to good advantage in other MGM releases like *See Here, Private Hargrove* and *Mrs. Parkington* (both 1944), *The Picture of Dorian Gray, They Were Expendable* (1945), *It's a Wonderful Life* (1946) and *Green Dolphin Street* (1947), where she became the embodiment of the perfectly sweet, ideal "girl next door."

After World War II, when audiences' tastes were beginning to change, Donna Reed was allowed to display her more versatile thespian abilities when she was cast against type as the prostitute Alma in Fred Zinnemann's highly-acclaimed World War II drama *From Here to Eternity* (1953) at Columbia, for which she took home the Best Supporting Actress Academy Award.

Later, there were some good occasional roles like *The Last Time I Saw Paris* a year later, but for the most part, her career in motion pictures seemed to be winding down. In 1958, after retiring from movies and concentrating on raising her family, she returned to acting when she accepted the role that made her a household name, perfect mother and housewife Donna Stone in the long-running television hit series *The Donna Reed Show* (1958–1966). Produced by her husband, Tony Owen, the series was a huge hit and continues to be rebroadcast on cable television to this day. After her series was cancelled, she made a few television movies and appeared on the hit series, *Dallas*, for one season (1984–85) as Miss Ellie Ewing. On January 14, 1986, Donna Reed passed away from pancreatic cancer.

Donna Reed films directed by John Ford:
They Were Expendable (1945)

Ward Bond (1903–1960)

Born Wardell Edwin Bond on April 9, 1903, in Benkelman, Nebraska, his family moved to Denver, Colorado, in 1919, where Ward graduated from East High School. While attending the University of Southern California, Ward was a starting lineman for USC's first national championship team when he met fellow player, John Wayne. The two became close friends and when director John Ford was casting some football players for his latest film, *Salute* (1929), for the Fox Film Corporation, he signed up the entire team. During filming, he was so impressed with both Ward Bond and John Wayne that he gave them odd jobs at the studio during the summer.

After a while, Ward Bond was bitten by the "acting bug" and worked in bit parts in pictures for a number of years. Eventually, he began getting speaking parts in films like *Arrowsmith* (1931), *Lady for a Day* (1933), *It Happened One Night* (1934), *Gone with the Wind* (1939), and many others. Soon, his career began to flourish and he would become one of the most durable character actors in motion pictures, appearing in more than 200 films throughout his lifetime, playing heavies, lawmen, fight promoters, cab drivers, or whatever the script called for. His most notable film credits would include *The Maltese Falcon* (1941), *Sergeant York* (1941), *Gentleman Jim* (1942), *It's a Wonderful Life* (1946), *Wagon Master* (1950), *The Quiet Man* (1952), *Mister Roberts* (1955) and *The Searchers* (1956).

Like John Wayne and Robert Montgomery, Ward Bond was a staunch conservative and could be very vocal both on and off the set, earning the ire of some of his colleagues. In the 1940s he joined the Motion Picture Alliance for the Preservation of American Ideals, which was a conservative group headed by John Wayne. Bond was not very well liked when he was later labeled as a rabid anti–Communist during the McCarthy era.

His fame peaked in 1957, when he was cast to star as wagon master Seth Andrews in the popular television series *Wagon Train*, which was inspired by the 1950 John Ford film, *Wagon Master*, in which Ward Bond co-starred. By the time he was doing the television series, Bond's rather belligerent demeanor had softened quite a bit and he seemed much more amiable to many of his young "guest stars" who appeared on the show. He died unexpectedly of a massive heart attack on November 5, 1960. His last theatrical release was Howard Hawks' *Rio Bravo* (1959), starring John Wayne.

Ward Bond films directed by John Ford:

Salute (1929)
Born Reckless (1930)
Up the River (1930)
Arrowsmith (1931)
Air Mail (1932)
Flesh (1932)
Submarine Patrol (1938)
Young Mr. Lincoln (1939)
Drums Along the Mohawk (1939)
The Grapes of Wrath (1940)
The Long Voyage Home (1940)
Tobacco Road (1941)
They Were Expendable (1945)
My Darling Clementine (1946)
The Fugitive (1947)
Fort Apache (1948)
Three Godfathers (1948)
Wagon Master (1950)
The Quiet Man (1952)
The Long Gray Line (1955)
Mister Roberts (1955)
The Searchers (1956)
The Wings of Eagles (1957)

V. The Celluloid Heroes and Supporting Cast

Jack Holt (1888–1951)

Charles John Holt was born in New York City on May 31, 1888. After moving with his parents to Winchester, Virginia, he attended the Virginia Military Institute but was expelled for misbehavior. Finding odd jobs as a gold prospector and a wrangler out west, he later landed a job as a stunt man in 1913. He caught the attention of cowboy star Francis Ford (brother of John Ford) and was eventually cast in his pictures, usually as a heavy. After appearing in some serials, his popularity began to flourish and his screen persona became that of a rugged, two-fisted leading man in action pictures. He was sometimes cast as a romantic lead. Well known for his angular face and distinctive profile (he was reportedly the model for the comic strip character, Dick Tracy, created by Chester Gould), he became a favorite of director Frank Capra, who cast him in three action pictures in the midst of the "talkie" revolution (*Submarine, Flight* and *Dirigible*).

After serving in both World Wars and rising to the rank of major, Holt went on playing supporting roles in movies until his death on January 18, 1951, following a massive heart attack. His two children, Tim and Jennifer, also became movie stars in their own right. Tim Holt, in particular, worked in many big productions, two of which, *Stagecoach* (1939) and *My Darling Clementine* (1946), were directed by John Ford, as well as starring in a series of B westerns. His most notable role came in 1948, when he was cast in the John Huston classic *The Treasure of the Sierra Madre*, starring Humphrey Bogart and Walter Huston. Tim received third billing and was outstanding as fellow prospector, Curtin. Jack Holt had a small, unnoticed cameo in the flophouse scene of that same movie.

Jack Holt films directed by John Ford:
They Were Expendable (1945)

Page from naval journal *The Chaser*, which gives an account of the location shooting of *They Were Expendable*. Sketches are by Carl Kidwell, who drew a sketch of Ward Bond on location.

Appendix 1—Promotion, Reviews and Critical Reception

Promotional Description from *The Motion Picture Exhibitor*, November 28, 1945

They Were Expendable

Estimate: well-made war tale rates high

Story: Prior to Pearl Harbor, the PT squadron at Manila evoked little attention from the Navy higher ups, and they were merely used for errands or pleasure over the protests of Lt. Robert Montgomery and Lt. (j.g.) John Wayne. After the attack on Pearl Harbor, they are given a chance to prove their worth, and come through on top once. Wayne is wounded and is shipped to a hospital, where he is cared for by army nurse Donna Reed. They fall in love. Their romance is broken up, however, when the PTs are ordered to evacuate high ranking officers to safety. At their new base, the boats turn again to knocking out Jap naval vessels and shipping. However, the remaining two boats of the squadron, captained by Wayne and Montgomery, are also shortly thereafter destroyed or rendered useless. The officers and crews are about to join General Jack Holt's men when they and two other officers are ordered to return to the U.S. to help train other PT crews. They go reluctantly.

X-ray: Although this is slightly dated, it still will be of tremendous inter-

Appendix 1

est to the thousands who read William White's book upon which the film is based as well as to those seeking a good war film with plenty of action. Performances by all concerned are top notch and are realistic as are the direction and production. The story is gripping throughout, and should find favor wherever shown. This rates high as entertainment, as a tribute to the PT branch of the Navy and to the *can-do* of Hollywood and the MGM studios.

Ad Lines: *Now it can be told ... the exciting story of the PT boats; Robert Montgomery, John Wayne, Donna Reed, and Jack Holt ... in the war's most exciting story ... They Were Expendable; never a story like it ... the heroic saga of the midget dynamite boats of World War II.*

Reviews and Critical Reception

"Now, with the war concluded and the byburning thirst for vengeance somewhat cooled, it comes as a cinematic postscript to the martial heat and passion of the last four years" (Bosley Crowther, *The New York Times*).

"John Ford had served in the navy, making several notable documentaries. This experience also added to the film's realism and poignancy, one of the finest of all WWII movies" (Polly Manguell, *501 Must-See Movies*).

"*They Were Expendable* was a major John Ford opus which seemed true to life (and death) in its account of torpedo boat crews fighting in the Jap dominated Pacific" (John Douglas Eames, *The M-G-M Story*).

"John Ford poured his accumulative emotions about WWII, a combination of personal bitterness and benign acceptance of duty, into this moving account of the fortunes of a PT-boat squadron as its ranks are thinned out during the loss of the Philippines" (Steven H. Scheuer, *Movies on TV*).

"A curious movie, whose premises Ford would obsessively rework in his subsequent cavalry pictures, with the luxury of historical distance" (Tom Milne, *The Time Out Film Guide*).

"Rather than a charging plot, *They Were Expendable* is a series of quotidian episodes moving unemphatically but inexorably toward nullity. For these are the little men who see only the war in front of them, and rarely see even that" (Tag Gallagher, *John Ford: The Man and His Films*).

Promotion, Reviews and Critical Reception

"The dichotomy of the formal beauty and classical composition with soft, romantic lighting of the scenes which allude to home, contrasted to the unstable, harshly dark world of the hospital and the other-worldly character of the battles, is reconciled in the last scene of the men on the beach" (J.A. Place, *The Non-Western Films of John Ford*).

"In the largely unspoken romance between John Wayne's Rusty and Donna Reed's nurse Sandy Davis, Ford captures a quality of muted longing that beautifully suggests the impossibility of sustaining any kind of satisfying relationship during the war" (Scott Eyman, *Print the Legend: The Life and Times of John Ford*).

"Informed with heightened emotion, a single shot, unexpectedly interposed—a ragged line of men marching into nowhere, one of them playing a bugle-call on his harmonica—assumes a deeper significance than is given by its function in the story. This is one of the properties of poetry. *They Were Expendable* is a heroic poem" (Lindsay Anderson, *About John Ford*).

"*They Were Expendable*'s verisimilitude, richness and texture, and sense of spontaneity are the by-product of Ford's three and a half years witnessing and recording actual warfare" (Joseph McBride, *Searching for John Ford*).

"One of the finest (and most underrated) of all WWII films, based on the true story of America's PT boat squadron in the Philippines during the early days of the war" (Leonard Maltin, *Leonard Maltin's Classic Movie Guide*).

APPENDIX 2—
KELLY V. LOEW'S, INC.

76 F.SUPP. 473 (1948)
Civ. A. No. 5071.
District Court, D. Massachusetts.

March 4, 1948.

Edward F. Flynn, Samuel Abrams and Garrett H. Byrne, all of Boston, Mass., for plaintiff. Nutter, McClennen & Fish and Edward F. McClennen, all of Boston, Mass., for defendant.

WYZANSKI, District Judge.

This is an action of libel brought by a commander of the United States Navy against the producer of the motion picture, They Were Expendable. The parties have waived a jury trial. The complaint refers first to the publication of the script of the cinema, and second to its exhibition at two Boston theatres, **Loew's** Orpheum and **Loew's** State, neither of which is owned by defendant. The gist of the three counts is that the portrayal of plaintiff, thinly disguised as the motion picture character, "Rusty Ryan," held him up to ridicule because it showed him engaging in conduct unbecoming an officer and gentleman. Particularly the script and the cinema are said to have shown him, in relation to naval officers and men, as headstrong, undisciplined, aggressive, resistant to orders and self-seeking, and in relation to a United States Army nurse, as unduly amorous. These portrayals are claimed to have damaged him by affecting his professional reputation and thus causing him embarrassment and mental discomfort.

Defendant's answer raises among other points that (1) the script was never published to any one; (2) defendant is not responsible for the showing of the motion picture in the Boston theatres; (3) there is no evidence that any one who saw the picture in Boston did identify Rusty Ryan with plaintiff; (4) neither the script nor the picture holds plaintiff up to ridicule in the eyes of any respectable part of the

Appendix 2

general public or even of the narrow circle of his own profession; and (5) plaintiff has given defendant a license to portray him as he was shown in the script and in the movie.

Plaintiff was born in New York City, and later lived in suburbs of New York and in Connecticut. He is admitted to be a citizen of one of the states of the United States other than Delaware, in which defendant is incorporated. From Connecticut he was appointed to the United States Naval Academy at Annapolis. He graduated from the Academy in 1935. In December 1941, having attained the rank of lieutenant in the United States Navy, he was stationed at the United States Naval Base at Cavite in the Philippines. At the time he was unmarried. He was the executive officer to Lieutenant Bulkeley commanding Motor Torpedo Boat Squadron Three, popularly referred to as PT boats. The relationship between plaintiff and Bulkeley was respectful and cordial but not intimate—first names never being used between them. PT boats of the type they commanded had by 1941 been used in active warfare by the British, Italian and other foreign navies, but our Navy had no occasion to use them in actual combat prior to the day of Pearl Harbor. There is, however, no reason for finding that in 1941 the United States Navy was skeptical about the usefulness of PT boats or that the persons, including plaintiff, who were assigned to duty aboard such ships regarded or had any occasion to regard the assignment either as unworthy of an able man or likely to limit his opportunities to serve his country or participate in engagements that tested a man's mettle, proficiency and courage.

In the weeks immediately preceding the attack on Pearl Harbor the PT boats in the Philippines, having received indirectly from the Commander-in-Chief warnings that war was imminent, were constantly on patrol. The night before the attack, after having performed his duties, plaintiff went to the Army and Navy Club for a hearty steak dinner, topped off with brandy and a cigar. Then he retired to his bachelor quarters to sleep. Between 2:30 and 4:30 a. m. he was awakened by news of the Japanese raid on Hawaii. Immediately he reported to duty and in the next few days was under fire from Japanese planes which attacked the Philippines. In these engagements he was not wounded. However, before hostilities had been declared his finger had swollen from the bite of a tropical insect, and after the war was under way plaintiff snagged his finger on some metal, probably on the ladder of one of the boats. (R. 91). He first showed his finger to his bowling companion who was a doctor. Then his commanding officer learned of the injury. After Pearl Harbor day, plaintiff was ordered by Lt. Bulkeley to the Army hospital at Corregidor (R. 102) where he was kept as a patient for about a month and to which during a second and a third month he was required to report as an outpatient two or three times a week. (R. 107, 108).

At the Army hospital there was an Army nurse, holding the rank of second lieutenant, named Peggy. She was one of about 14 nurses assigned to Corregidor where there were approximately eleven thousand men. She was a girl in her twenties of moderate girth and height who wore glasses and who while perhaps not accurately described as "cute" was undeniably attractive to the men at Corregidor.

When plaintiff entered the hospital he fell under the care of Peggy, whose authority or rank he never challenged. From time to time thereafter she ministered to his medical needs. Plaintiff and Peggy became friendly but there is no evidence that there was any romantic attachment or any amorous intimacy. They never ate together except in the hospital. (R. 108). On occasions after plaintiff's discharge from the hospital they went for walks together. And after plaintiff left Cavite, Peggy wrote some letters to him and possibly he wrote to her; but the letters were not in evidence or demanded for production.

After plaintiff was discharged from the hospital he participated in naval engagements of historic importance. The squadron of which Lt. Bulkeley was commander and plaintiff executive officer was assigned tasks of major significance, and never was limited to messenger duty or like routine tasks. In view of the small size of the boats and the limited availability of torpedoes, fuel oil and like supplies, the PT boats performed incredible feats of warfare.

In March 1942, the PT boats were given a mission that became world famous. Lt. Bulkeley, plaintiff and others carried from Cavite to Mindanao General MacArthur, his wife, their son, Admiral Rockwell and other high military and naval personnel. Plaintiff commanded the PT boat which transported Admiral Rockwell. The skill and bravery with which this mission was performed earned each of the PT officers and men the Silver Star.

After arriving at Mindanao the Motor Torpedo Boats continued their superb work of slowing and diminishing the effectiveness of the Japanese advance. It is possible that one of the exploits of Lt. **Kelly's** boat was the sinking of a Japanese cruiser of the Kuma class. Eyewitnesses ashore believed they saw the cruiser sink, but later reports of naval engagements involving the particular cruiser thought to have been sunk cast some doubt upon the reports of the eyewitnesses. Whatever may be the truth with respect to this particular incident, there is no room for controversy regarding the over-all naval success of the squadron, the danger which the officers and men faced, the casualties they bore and the heroism with which they responded in the nation's most critical hour.

Plaintiff could well testify—though unlike Aeneas he would never volunteer the statement—"Quaeque ipse miserrima vidi, Et quorum para magna fui" (II Aeneid 5). Indeed if one were to select for special notice any particular event in the history of the squadron, the selection made by defendant's attorney could hardly be bettered. Returning from a battle plaintiff's boat became fouled with some coral heads. It was attacked by four Japanese seaplanes (R. 21). The planes killed

Appendix 2

or injured all except plaintiff and three other members of the crew (R. 22). Plaintiff helped ashore his wounded companions, but the Japanese planes continued strafing the survivors. Acting with incredible presence of mind, dispatch and gallantry plaintiff beached his boat and saved some of his wounded companions (R. 22). Those who had been lost in the battle were buried in an Anglo-American cemetery after a funeral service performed by a priest but unattended by plaintiff who had other duties to fulfill.

In the spring of 1942 the United States Navy, desiring that its officers and men in the United States should have training in the use of motor torpedo boats by officers familiar with their value in active combat, ordered Lt. Bulkeley, plaintiff and others to the naval training station at Melville, Rhode Island. (R. 79). The transportation from Mindanao was by airplane, and there was no time at which plaintiff offered or thought of offering to disregard his orders and surrender to another the airplane seat which he had been directed to occupy. On arrival in the United States and before reporting to Rhode Island, plaintiff was given a ten-day leave. He went to the home of his mother, who had moved to New York City from Connecticut. After three or four days, the Office of Public Relations of the United States Department of the Navy discovered that plaintiff was in New York City. Despite his own reluctance and because persons holding superior rank in the Navy made it clear that plaintiff should cooperate, plaintiff participated in a parade and two banquets in New York City intended not only as a testimonial of honor to the heroes of the PT boats but also as part of a promotional campaign to sell United States Savings Bonds. (R. 80, 82). This type of display was so out of character with plaintiff's natural disposition that he voluntarily terminated his own leave several days ahead of time and reported for duty at the naval training station in Rhode Island. (R. 26).

Hardly had he reached there when plaintiff was requested by an official of the United States Navy to allow himself to be interviewed by William L. White—a reputable and widely known reporter then on the staff of the periodical, Reader's Digest. (Ex. 1, R. 27, 86). Plaintiff understood that he and his fellow survivors of the PT boats were to tell their stories so that Mr. White could write a factual account for the magazine. For three and one-half days for six or seven hours a day Mr. White asked plaintiff questions. (R. 28). And at the end Mr. White left the station without showing his manuscript or even his notes to plaintiff. (R. 162).

In September or October 1942 plaintiff received an advance copy of a book called They Were Expendable written by William L. White and published by Harcourt, Brace & Co. (R. 88). The book begins with a foreword stating that the author was told the story "largely in the officers' quarters of the Motor Torpedo Boat Station at Melville, Rhode Island, by four young officers"; "because the navy was then keeping him [Lt. Bulkeley] so busy fulfilling his obligations as a national hero,

Kelly v. Loew's, Inc.

Bulkeley had to delegate to Lieutenant Robert Bolling **Kelly** a major part of the task of rounding out the narrative. I think the reader will agree that the choice was wise, for Lieutenant **Kelly**, in addition to being a brave and competent naval officer, has a sense of narrative and a keen eye for significant detail, two attributes which may never help him in battle but which were of great value to this book." And at the end of the book there is a three page table of the real names of the "officers and enlisted personnel attached to motor torpedo boat squadron three." Thus the book purports to be and in fact is a substantially accurate report of "historical events"— as that phrase is used in the letter of December 21, 1942 (Ex. 4) to which reference is made later in this opinion. However, there is in the book some mild profanity which I attribute not to plaintiff but to Mr. White's sense of fitness.

The White book describes with historical fidelity the way news of the Pearl Harbor disaster reached Cavite; the early activities of PT boats; the hospitalization of plaintiff rendering him unable to participate in certain early encounters; plaintiff's role in a Subic Bay enterprise in which Lt. Bulkeley sank a 10,000 ton tanker; the transportation of General MacArthur's party; General MacArthur's promise to get Lt. Bulkeley and other key men out of the Philippines; Lt. Bulkeley's later transportation of President Quezon; the repair of plaintiff's boat; the episode of the possible sinking of a Japanese cruiser of the Kuma class by torpedoes from plaintiff's boat; the beaching and destruction of the boat at Kawit Island; plaintiff's gallantry in saving his men and crew; the report of the burial mass conducted by a priest after plaintiff had departed; plaintiff's hope that General MacArthur would fulfil his promise to get him out of the Philippines; and the final flight from the Philippine airport to Australia.

Two aspects of the White account require special attention—the author's portrayal of plaintiff's relations to Peggy and of plaintiff's character as an officer.

Mr. White shows the lieutenant and nurse as friendly in a perfectly proper way, and yet with an affectionate concern for one another. Lt. **Kelly's** first impression of Peggy was that she had "a cute way of telling you very firmly what you had to do" (p. 29). They became companions and they had dates, went together to a party or two and at least once sat at the mouth of Corregidor's tunnel where "every five minutes an army truck would barge tactlessly around the curve" (p. 61). Before he left with the MacArthur party she called him over the signal-corps phone and though he couldn't tell her his mission, he said "I guess it's good-bye, Peggy" (p. 117). Often after they separated his mind went back to her, her plight at Bataan and memories of her gifts of food and drugs for an emergency. As he boarded the airplane to go to Australia he "remembered the last thing she said to me—her voice was just as clear as if it had been two seconds ago, instead of many weeks, over that signal-corps telephone in the army hut on Bataan after I had told her this was good-bye. 'Well,' she said, 'it's been awfully nice, hasn't it.'" (p. 205).

Appendix 2

Mr. White shows plaintiff as a man of magnificent courage and deep feeling but at no time out of control of himself. This self-restraint is indeed almost a salient characteristic. Thus when, accompanied by a colonel, plaintiff was sent to report to a general at the American Club the important news of the loss of the PT boat and some of his men, and of the PT's sinking of a Japanese cruiser, he was kept waiting an unconscionable time. Though the plaintiff got mad, apparently inside, he does not appear to have moved a muscle externally except to go over and have a Coca-Cola with the colonel. (p. 178). Another time when an army colonel assigned him the duty of leading fifty carabao—that is, milk cows—after they were rounded up, plaintiff "didn't say much"; he waited to see if the order would not be superseded by his right to take the expected plane; and by waiting, the conflict was avoided. (p. 197). In short, Mr. White's impression—like the one I myself gathered from plaintiff's appearance in court—is that he has unusual steadiness of temper.

Since the true names of the plaintiff and the others were set forth in the foreword and in the body of Mr. White's book, I find that their names and identities became widely known in book-reading communities, such as Boston and its suburbs.

Recognizing the dramatic value of the book, a score of representatives of motion picture producers approached plaintiff, who was still on duty in the continental United States, to secure his permission to portray his character and exploits on the screen. Plaintiff repeatedly refused. I find that his primary reason was his natural reserve and distaste for self-advertisement; his secondary and distinctly minor reason was that the publicity might operate to prejudice his professional career. To meet that second objection, Honorable Frank Knox, a former newspaper publisher, then Secretary of the Navy, on December 15, 1942 wrote a letter directly to plaintiff stating that the proposed motion picture "seems to be for the best interests of the Navy Department. A copy of this letter has been forwarded to the Bureau of Personnel for inclusion in your official record" [Ex. 3]. Reading between the lines of that letter, plaintiff understood and I conclude that a reasonable person would have understood that the letter was the equivalent not of a command but of a peremptory preference carrying overtones of possible consequences if the writer's pleasure or displeasure were awakened by the recipient's reaction.

Even after receiving Secretary Knox's letter, plaintiff desired to limit the license which he would give defendant as the producer of the motion picture, They Were Expendable. He rejected various drafts of a proposed license which were submitted to him. (R. 116). Finally, on December 21, 1942, he signed a letter which he did not write and which was submitted to him by the Office of Public Relations of the United States Navy which in this instance was, I find, acting on behalf of the motion picture producer which was the intended beneficiary of the license. The text of the letter is as follows:

Kelly v. Loew's, Inc.

(Undated) "**Loew's** Incorporated 1540 Broadway New York, N. Y.

Dear Sirs: —

I am one of the Navy officers of whom Mr. White wrote in his book 'They Were Expendable.' You are proposing to produce this book, or your version of it, in motion pictures and television and radio performances, but the law in some of the states is that before you impersonate me or use a character that would correspond to me, you need my approval. I now waive, as to you and your assigns and licensees, all personal rights and objections to any use to be made of me or my personality which has the approval of the United States Navy. If the Navy approves, then so far as I am concerned I can be depicted or a character used that may correspond to me, in pictures, radio and television performances and their publicity, with such action, depiction, dialogue and story (fictional or actual), as passes Navy approval. As to name, any name except my exact name can be used for this character that meets Navy approval, even if it is similar to my real name.

This release is granted by me subject to your agreement that the romance shall not be elaborated beyond the portrayal of it in the book and, if possible, shall be played down; and that the historical events in the picture shall be portrayed as accurately as possible in such a screen dramatization.

Yours very truly, s/ Robert B. **Kelly**"

Some time passed and plaintiff's mind was on matters far removed from the motion picture world. On May 28, 1944 plaintiff married Miss Hazel Babcock Watts, who was living with her parents in their home in Malden, Massachusetts. He secured a short leave and he and his bride spent part of their honeymoon, perhaps a fortnight, in her parents' home. He met then, as he had met previously when he was courting his future wife, her family and friends who were living in the Greater Boston area.

Afterwards plaintiff and his wife went to Florida where he was officially stationed. In that Florida neighborhood defendant happened to be taking some of the "shots" for the film, They were Expendable. Plaintiff's recollection being refreshed by hearing of that enterprise, he determined to call upon defendant's officers at Culver City, California, when, a few weeks later, he and his wife were in San Diego preparatory to plaintiff's departing for the Far East to participate in the Okinawa campaign and occupation.

On arriving in California in February 1945, plaintiff conferred with Messrs. Wead and Reed, employees of defendant. Wead was a former commander in the United States Navy who, after having been crippled in service, retired to become an employee of defendant in producing motion pictures concerned with naval subjects. Wead and Reed sent for the script of They Were Expendable. Both of them examined it. (R. 53). One of them, probably Reed, handed the script to the other, probably Wead, who in turn handed it to plaintiff. Wead expressed confidence that plaintiff would be satisfied with the script and suggested that plaintiff should notify him if he had any comments.

Appendix 2

On returning to his hotel, plaintiff hastily leaved through the pages of the script. He read perhaps a third or a quarter of it, and up to then found nothing that gave him pain. In the confusion of departure, the script was put in Mrs. **Kelly's** bag, not in plaintiff's. Later Mrs. **Kelly** sent the script to her husband but he did not read it until June, 1945, after the Okinawa campaign. At once he wrote a letter of protest to defendant. Defendant's representative replied that the picture had reached the cutting stage and that it was too late to alter it, but that the representative was confident that plaintiff would be satisfied.

In January 1946, the motion picture, They Were Expendable, as produced by defendant, was exhibited in **Loew's** State and **Loew's** Orpheum in Boston and was seen by large crowds—though there is no evidence as to any particular person or class of persons who attended the performances. Following the showing plaintiff was in the Greater Boston area and at social and like gatherings he often felt embarrassment, uneasiness and self-consciousness in seeing such acquaintances and meeting such new persons as had seen the portrayal of him in the movie. (R. 67).

At some unspecified time, whether before or after the showing of the movie does not appear, plaintiff was awarded the Navy Cross and a number of other unsolicited medals, including the Silver Star medal with Gold Star in lieu of second award, the China Service medal, the American Defense medal, the American Theatre of Operations medal, the Asiatic-Pacific Theatre of Operations medal and the World War II Victory medal (R. 68). Also on his own application he was in 1946 awarded the Purple Heart on account of the snagged finger which led to his hospitalization. Since the summer of 1946 and pursuant to orders issued in May 1946, plaintiff has been serving as an instructor in the Department of Marine Engineering at Annapolis. (R. 69). He has in the meantime attained the permanent rank of Commander in the United States Navy.

The picture, They Were Expendable, opens with the statements that it is based upon the book, They Were Expendable, by William L. White, and that it was produced under the direction of Commander John Ford, U.S.N., and with the corporation and assistance of the United States Navy. It concludes with a list of the characters, of which in the order given by defendant, the first is "Lt. Brickley" played by Robert Montgomery and the second is "Lt. 'Rusty' Ryan" played by John Wayne. And there is the customary legend that "The events, characters and firms depicted in this photoplay are fictitious. Any similarity to actual persons, living or dead, or to actual firms is purely coincidental."

Between the start and the end of the film the story is given in the following form. The PT boats were a new venture in 1941. Regular naval officers looked upon them with skepticism. But Brickley had great faith in them and had induced his intimate friend, Ryan, to stake his career on their future. When first reviewed by high officers in the Philippines, the squadron received such a cold reception that

Kelly v. Loew's, Inc.

Ryan decided that Brickley was overenthusiastic and that the PT boats would never be recognized for their value. Immediately he went to a bar to write out his request for transfer from PT duty to destroyer duty. He was about to present the request when the announcement came in the bar that Pearl Harbor had been attacked. Ryan at once changed his mind and tore up the request for a change of assignment. They both reported to the admiral in charge of Cavite. He then gave the PT boats only messenger and ferry service. Ryan was put out; kicked a can in disgust; and showed general displeasure. However, he remained with the squadron. And shortly afterwards while dining with his fellows, he and they heard a Japanese air attack coming. All hurried to the PT boats, put them out to sea, and at once were bombed by Japanese planes. In this engagement Ryan got shrapnel in his arm.

At first Ryan ignored the arm wound. One day he and Brickley were summoned by the admiral to discuss an important combat task. Both received assignments. Ryan proposed to ignore his wound. Brickley, however, became aware of its importance and sent him to the Corregidor hospital. An attractive, slim nurse, holding the rank of second lieutenant and named "'Sandy' Davis," ordered him to lie down and put on a blanket. At first Ryan objected and inquired as to her rank. She reminded him of her authority as a nurse. He obeyed, lay down and covered himself with a blanket. She and an orderly pulled off his trousers in a perfectly proper way. There seemed to be no sympathy between the nurse and Ryan. Another patient who was an onlooker said that every man in the hospital was fond of Sandy.

Some days later there was a dance to give the nurses some recreation. Initially Ryan, when asked by Sandy, said he didn't dance and wouldn't go to the dance. After strains of music reached him, Ryan strolled over to the dance hall. Sandy asked him if he really didn't dance. He said he did. They danced and then they went out on a porch and sat down. In the picture she nestled close to him. In the tradition of the third chapter of Genesis, the female took the lead. But so far as defendant's film shows, Ryan did no more than offer a comforting arm and hand.

The film then showed plaintiff returning to PT duty. His boat as well as others participated in stirring naval engagements, including the battle with the Japanese cruiser and the later bombardment and destruction of Ryan's PT boat by Japanese planes. In one of these scenes Ryan acts heroically saving his wounded companion from strafing by Japanese seaplanes. After that attack has concluded there is a funeral for those of Ryan's crew who died. No priest is available. So the survivors assemble in a Catholic church where Ryan as senior officer conducts the service by saying a few words and reciting a moving poem. An enlisted man, after requesting Ryan's permission, plays "Taps" on his harmonica. Overcome with emotion, Ryan leaves during the final notes of "Taps" and rushes to a neighboring bar. The proprietor is about to close for the day. Ryan seizes a bottle of liquor from the

Appendix 2

proprietor's basket, makes him re-open the bar, sits down at a table and pours out two drinks for himself. Others of the crew drink at the main bar.

In one of the intervals between the battles comes the assignment of Brickley and Ryan to carry from the Philippines dignitaries whose identity is not at first disclosed. As they are about to leave Cavite, Ryan tries to get Sandy on the telephone to say good-bye. They start talking but the connection is interrupted by the wires being torn down by army officers or men. Ryan goes to his boat. One of his juniors has the helm. When Ryan sees who the dignitaries are, he shoves his junior aside and takes the wheel. The boats safely transport the principal personages, General MacArthur and his family and an Admiral called "Blackwell."

Finally there is an order from Washington directing Brickley, Ryan and two others to return to the United States to discuss with high naval officials the value of PT boats and their performance. Brickley and Ryan are reluctant to leave their associates who have not been similarly removed from danger. But they nonetheless bid their companions farewell in a moving scene in which the Chief Boatswain's Mate who is left behind wounded says "The book doesn't mean much out here so I'm going to say: So long Brick. You've been a swell guy." Brickley replies: "So long, Irish." The Chief Boatswain's Mate Mulcahey says "So long, Rusty." Ryan answers: "So long, you big Mick."

Arrived at the airport, Brickley and Ryan are given seats 27 and 28 in a plane with space for 30. At first the men who should receive spaces 29 and 30 do not appear. Two substitutes are seated. Then, as the plane is about to take off, the men originally assigned for seats 29 and 30 arrive. One of the substitutes as he leaves gives Ryan a message for home. Ryan impulsively offers the substitute his seat and says he, Ryan, "has business" still to do in the Philippines—by which the audience might infer either that Ryan wants to continue fighting or that Ryan has to see Sandy. Brickley intervenes sharply asking Ryan "Who're you working for—yourself." The picture comes to an end.

In substance, the script which was given to plaintiff in California in February, 1945, does not diverge sharply from the final motion picture. There are in the script some more romantic scenes—including one in which Ryan puts his and Sandy's name inside a heart he draws (R. 61, Ex. 5, Sc. 241, p. 92)—and the language and conduct of Ryan toward his fellow officers and his men is a shade more colorful and unrestrained. But for reasons which will become apparent in the course of this opinion I need not dwell on these minor discrepancies.

Looked at in the broadest way, both the film and the script depict Ryan as a gallant officer, zealous to serve the nation, respectful of his superiors, companionable with his equals, considerate of his men, responsive—but not too responsive—to the charms of women. He has the striking virtues of his race—kindliness, generosity, humor, love of his fellow men, impetuous eagerness for action, exuberance of spirit. He is the sort of man that crowds like because they admire his virtues and condone his faults. They see the brave heart of the hero, the sportsmanship of the open fighter, the quick emotion of the sensitive man. And if they also see hastiness, occasional intemperance, minor infractions of rules, impatience at official blindness, they regard those as being not faults at all or the sort of faults which are the mark of the man of courageous action, the man of large heart, the man who lives by the spirit and not by the letter.

But Ryan appears somewhat differently if he is looked at in the tradition of the professional class of naval officers. He then appears an undisciplined man. Discontented with a PT boat assignment which seems to lead neither to glory nor the grave, he impatiently prepares a request for transfer. He gives vent to his feelings by kicking around cans. He reprimands men in public. He resents and at first resists the authority which an army nurse has over a patient in any army hospital. He shoves a man away from the helm of his boat. He loses his composure when conducting ceremonies for the dead. He seeks consolation for his grief not merely by going to a bar, but by requiring the bar-keep to remain open and by seizing from his possession a bottle of liquor. He fraternizes with his commanding officer and with his men. He is, until reminded of his duty, prepared to ignore the order that he return to the United States merely so that he can attend to his own personal business with a girl. Viewed from the professional aspect Ryan may be a hard fighter of noble character, but he does not measure up to the, shall I say, "regulation" model of a good officer.

On the facts as I have just stated them, these are my conclusions of law.

1. This case is properly removed into the United States District Court on the basis of diversity of citizenship. I find that plaintiff is a citizen of Massachusetts (R. 35), and defendant a Delaware corporation, and there is at stake a controversy involving, exclusive of costs and interest, more than $3,000.

2. In this proceeding I am required to follow the principles of conflict of laws which prevail in the state courts of Massachusetts. Klaxon Co. v. Stentor Co., 313 U.S. 487, 61 S.Ct. 1020, 85 L.Ed. 1477; Hartmann v. Time, Inc., 3 Cir., 166 F.2d 127. The ordinary rule of conflicts invoked by Massachusetts in tort cases is to apply the law of the place of the wrong. Murphy v. Smith, 307 Mass. 64, 29 N.E.2d 726; National Fruit Product Co. v. Dwinell-Wright Co., D.C.Mass., 47 F.Supp. 499, 504.

There is no difficulty in applying that ordinary rule to count 1. That related solely to the script; and at the trial the only evidence offered of a showing of the script was evidence of a showing in California. Thus California law would be applied by Massachusetts to that transaction. Murphy v. Smith, supra.

Greater complexity arises in connection with counts 2 and 3. Complaint was made in those counts and evidence was received on those counts with respect to

Appendix 2

showings of the film itself solely in two Massachusetts theatres during specified weeks.

If complaint had been made of showings not only in Massachusetts, but elsewhere, the Massachusetts court would have been clearly faced with the need of determining whether to regard the conduct complained of as a single tort [see, for example, the Pennsylvania rule referred to in Hartmann v. Time, supra] or as multiple torts [see, for example, Hartmann v. American News Co., D.C.Wis., 69 F.Supp. 736, 738, 739]. If it took the single tort view the Massachusetts court would presumably regard as "the publication" not the circulation of the script (which admittedly differed from the movie), nor the circulation of the "continuity" of the film, nor the first showing of the picture to the producer's employees, but rather the first showing of the picture to the public. Then the Massachusetts court would have to determine whether the law to be applied to that "publication" was the law of the place of production, or the law of the place of the first showing of the film to the general public, or the law of plaintiff's domicil, or the law of the place where plaintiff enjoyed his principal reputation, or some other law. Note, 60 Harv.L.Rev. 941. See also 59 Harv.L.Rev. 136. So far as I am aware, the law books give no indication how the Massachusetts state courts would decide any of the issues referred to in this paragraph in a case where complaint was made of multiple showings in many states. Indeed, Massachusetts has never indicated whether multiple showings in a single state constitute one or several torts. Holmes, J., specifically reserved the question in Bigelow v. Sprague, 140 Mass. 425, 428, lines 8, 9, 5 N.E. 144, 146: "whether the publication of the edition is to be regarded technically as, so to speak, one composite act, we need not consider."

To be sure, the complaint at bar is limited to showings in Massachusetts alone. The mere fact that the complaint is so limited does not as a matter of logic avoid the problem stated in the preceding paragraph. In other words, logically the Massachusetts court must decide whether such local showings are or are not a part of a composite multi-state tort. The only time the Massachusetts court faced up to that logic it ruled that such local showings were not a part of a single multi-state tort. Commonwealth v. Blanding, 1825, 3 Pick. 304, 311, 15 Am.Dec. 214. In that case defendant printed a defamatory newspaper in Rhode Island, and circulated it there and in Massachusetts. A criminal proceeding was brought in Massachusetts on account of the circulation in Massachusetts. It was held by the Supreme Judicial Court that a separate publication occurred in Massachusetts and was criminally punishable under the law of Massachusetts. This case can of course be distinguished. First, it is a criminal case where local policies may have peculiar force. Second, it is a case which was decided in an age unfamiliar with mass media of circulation such as our modern periodicals, motion pictures and radio broadcasts. Despite these distinctions the case has been followed recently and is sometimes cited for the proposition that a circulation of alleged defamatory material within Massachusetts subjects the circulator to the rules of Massachusetts law.

Indeed, the cases in the United States District Court for Massachusetts based upon its diversity jurisdiction go far to sustain the proposition just stated. Thus in O'Reilly v. Curtis Pub. Co., D.C.Mass., 31 F.Supp. 364, 365, Judge Brewster treated the circulations in Massachusetts (1) as separate from those in Rhode Island and (2) apparently as constituting a composite. "The publication in each of the thirty-eight states gives rise to separate causes of action. The defendant's liability for the libel published in each state is governed by the laws of that particular state. For example, the publication in Rhode Island would support a separate action * * *." In Wright v. R. K. O. Radio Pictures, D.C.Mass., 55 F.Supp. 639, a libel suit in which plaintiff complained only of publications in Massachusetts, though the publication involved a motion picture which had been nationally distributed, Judge Sweeney applied Massachusetts law. In McGlue v. Weekly Publications Inc., D. C.Mass., 63 F.Supp. 744, where complaint was made of circulations in many states Judge Sweeney applied the Massachusetts Statute of Limitations apparently on the theory that all circulation inside and outside Massachusetts was a composite wrong which occurred on the day of the first circulation in Massachusetts. In Curley v. Curtis Pub. Co., D.C.Mass., 48 F.Supp. 29, 30, note 3, where there was a jury trial of a Massachusetts citizen's complaint alleging the circulation in 48 states of an alleged defamatory statement I applied the law of Massachusetts.

The foregoing authorities seem to me to justify my concluding that the Massachusetts rule is that where a person who is domiciled in Massachusetts and whose chief reputation is not shown to have any particular locus complains in Massachusetts of only the circulation within Massachusetts of an alleged defamatory statement, the court applies Massachusetts law. This rule has the merit of simplicity, of readiness in ascertaining the governing precedents and statutes, and of applying the standard of the community where plaintiff's reputation is presumably most affected. This rule does not necessarily imply that every circulation in Massachusetts is part of one composite act, nor that every circulation outside of Massachusetts is part of the same composite act as the circulations in Massachusetts. Such implications might be logically sound and consistent with the rational of the rule as I have stated it. But decision on those implications should await an appropriate case. Before that case arises the problem may be dealt with by local or federal statute. Surely no problem more imperatively requires the attention of those interested in the combined field of torts and conflict of laws.

3. With respect to the script the first serious issue is whether there was any publication at all. On the view of the evidence most favorable to plaintiff the script was shown by defendant to Wead, to Reed, and to clerical, production, theatrical and other internal employees of **Loew's**. (Of course, the showing to Mrs. **Kelly** was only by plaintiff, not by defendant.) Publication by one employee of a corporation to another employee has been squarely held by the Massachusetts court to be a publication sufficient for the purposes of a libel suit. Bander v. Metropol-

Appendix 2

itan Life Ins. Co., 313 Mass. 337, 348, 349, 47 N.E.2d 595. But the precise issue is whether the same ruling would be made by the courts of the state of California. There appears to be no direct California authority. However, since I am sitting in a diversity jurisdiction case removed from the Massachusetts state courts, since the Massachusetts rule treats an intracorporate communication of a defamatory statement as a publication, since Massachusetts presumes in the absence of evidence to the contrary that California's common law is like its own [Cormo v. Boston Bridge Works, 205 Mass. 366, 368, 91 N. E. 313] and since Restatement, Torts, § 577, comment (e) and a number of recent cases collated in 166 A.L.R. 114, lend themselves to support of the Massachusetts rule, I shall conclude for the purpose of this case that California also treats an intra-corporate communication of a defamatory statement as a publication.

4. However, the script was published only to persons in the motion picture industry. Even Wead was an employee only of defendant, not of the Navy. And a central question is, if we assume that they identified plaintiff with the character Ryan, was their opinion of him or his reputation lowered or likely to be lowered in any way by reading the script? We are in this aspect of the case concerned with what would be the opinion not of the general public nor of naval officers, nor of plaintiff himself, but of persons in the motion picture industry. There is no reason to believe that persons in that industry are peculiarly sensitive to standards of naval discipline, official propriety and etiquette. Nor is there ground for supposing that they hold cool detachment in higher esteem than warmth of heart, vigor of expression and display of intensity of feeling. Hence to that audience the publication of the script—including love scenes somewhat more torrid than those that finally appeared on the screen—was not the publication of anything that held plaintiff up to contempt, hatred or ridicule in their eyes or that lowered their estimate of plaintiff's reputation. To that audience it was not a defamatory statement. Cf. Restatement, Torts, § 559, comment (e), p. 142, lines 3–9; § 569, comment (d); § 614(2).

5. Nor on this record can it be successfully contended that regardless of the views of persons in the motion picture industry, the script was defamatory per se because it depicted plaintiff as engaged in unlawful conduct. It is conceivable that Rusty Ryan by action, gesture or word, may have violated a regulation adopted by the Navy pursuant to statute, and may thus have committed an offense punishable by court-martial. But the pleadings and the testimony at bar point to no such violation. It is not the task of the Court to search out every naval regulation, to consider whether any part of Ryan's conduct offends that regulation and then to decide whether the insinuation of such offence is for purposes of a libel suit to be regarded as the charge of a crime of the type which if oral makes a statement defamatory per se. Bander v. Metropolitan Life Ins. Co., 313 Mass. 337, 341, 47 N.E.2d 595. Cf. Restatement, Torts, § 571, comment on clause (a), p. 173.

6. Now I turn from the script to the motion picture itself. Defendant first contends that it is not accountable for the showing of the picture at the two Boston theatres referred to in the complaint. If I understand counsel's argument, it is that one who produces an allegedly defamatory motion picture for exhibition and who distributes it to an exhibitor, is not liable for the injury inflicted by that particular exhibitor's showing. This argument is so preposterous as hardly to require answer and certainly not citation of extensive rebutting authority. The producer intended the very exhibition that occurred. It was not a performance independent of its will but the ultimate end toward which the whole production was directed. That the final exhibitor was technically an independent contractor not an agent of the producer is irrelevant. Merchants' Ins. Co. of Newark, N. J. v. Buckner, 6 Cir., 98 F. 222, 230, 231; Restatement, Torts, § 577, comment (f).

7. If counsel means to imply that defendant is not accountable at bar because plaintiff has embraced in his suit only the injury suffered from the showing in two theatres in Boston and has not embraced other injuries suffered from other showings, also caused by defendant directly, or through agents, or through independent contractors, the answer is equally plain. There is no obligation to complain of all the damages caused by defendant. However, if because of the doctrine of "composite torts" the damages not claimed are part of the same cause of action as the damages that were claimed, then of course a new action will not lie for the unclaimed damages.

8. Defendant next makes the point that plaintiff failed to bear the burden of showing that the audiences in the Boston theatre identified him with the character Rusty Ryan. Physically they did not look alike, as the Court could see by comparing the motion picture with the plaintiff when he was on the stand. Emotionally they did not resemble one another—plaintiff being a man of far greater reserve, composure and dignity. Nominally they were distinguishable—Ryan does not sound like **Kelly**. But all these distinctions are beside the point. The motion picture recited that it was based on William L. White's book, They Were Expendable; and that book throughout uses **Kelly's** true name and the author in the foreward and elsewhere makes it plain that **Kelly** is a living officer identical with plaintiff in this suit. Thus by giving the key—if key were needed—to unlock the mysteries of the picture defendant plainly asked the audience to believe—and I conclude that many of them did believe—that Ryan in the movie was substantially like **Kelly** in life. The disingenuous legend that the persons and events shown in the picture were fictitious and that any similarity to actual persons living or dead was purely coincidental would not have been treated by the average person or naval officer as any more than a tongue-in-the-cheek disclaimer in view of the express reference by the movie to Mr. White's book, in view of the statement of Navy cooperation and in view of the unmistakable portrayal of General MacArthur, his family and other historic personages, including both Lt. Bulkeley and plaintiff.

Appendix 2

9. Related to the last point, defendant seems to suggest that there is no showing that anyone in the Boston audiences personally knew Commander **Kelly** in 1946. If this is the suggestion, it is without merit. The question is not whether the audience knew Commander **Kelly** personally, but whether they knew his reputation. That his reputation was known in Boston is demonstrable in two alternative ways: first, his exploits had been reported in Mr. White's best-selling non-fiction book; and second, his exploits had been reported over the radio (Ex. 2, p. 198) and were well known in large cities. Thus in New York City, where he had not lived at least since infancy and which had therefore no reason to have a greater knowledge than Boston would have of him, he was the feature attraction of a parade and two banquets intended to promote the sale of government bonds. Moreover, one would have to be peculiarly blind to the racial and religious composition of Greater Boston, to the understandable pride that every group takes in heroes drawn from backgrounds like its own, and to the conspicuous record which plaintiff had made in the Navy to suppose that Commander **Kelly** was entirely unknown to the audiences at the State and Orpheum theatres in Boston.

10. I now turn to what is to my mind the most difficult problem in this case—did the motion picture of They Were Expendable shown at the Boston theatres cause the audiences in those theatres to have a lower opinion of Commander **Kelly**—did it affect his reputation by causing him to be held up to contempt, hatred or ridicule?

The romantic incidents of Ryan's career certainly could not bring Commander **Kelly** into even a Puritan's ridicule or disesteem. Ryan's conduct toward ladies would have been becoming to anyone, sailor or civilian, officer or man. His conduct on duty, however, raises more subtle issues. And in resolving them it is important to emphasize one consideration of law and another of fact.

In deciding whether a statement is defamatory, the rule is to determine what its effect is upon any respectable, substantial part of the community to which the statement was addressed. Thus if the community or audience includes a professional group to which the subject of the statement belongs, the question is the effect of the statement upon that group with its special professional standards. Mr. Justice Holmes gave an apt illustration in Peck v. Tribune Co., 214 U.S. 185, where he said at page 190, 29 S.Ct. 554, at page 556, 53 L.Ed. 960, 16 Ann.Cas. 1075, "If a doctor were represented as advertising, the fact that it would effect his standing with others of his profession might make the representation actionable, although advertising is not reputed dishonest and even seems to be regarded by many with pride." See accord Restatement, Torts, § 559(e).

And in applying that rule of law to the case at bar, we are to remember that the showing complained of was in January, 1946—a mere four months after hostilities had ceased and at a period when this Court takes judicial notice that the Port of

Kelly v. Loew's, Inc.

Boston was crowded with permanent officers of the United States Navy, some of whom it may reasonably be inferred went to a motion picture in the production of which the Navy cooperated.

Thus the issue narrowly stated is whether to permanent officers of the United States Navy the portrayal of plaintiff as resembling Ryan would tend to lower his reputation. In the light of the lack of evidence that Annapolis men were in the audience it would not seem proper to confine the professional group whose opinion we are testing to the narrow circle of those who had graduated from the Naval Academy. And obviously it would be improper to use plaintiff's personal reaction except so far as it is typical of any naval officer's reaction as the test whether the portrayal held him up to contempt, hatred or ridicule.

The testimony warrants this Court in finding and the Court finds that as a group naval officers like other professional groups, such as doctors, lawyers or judges have a standard of judgment of their colleagues which is peculiar to their profession and which differs sharply from the appraisal of the uninitiated. (Cf.R. 8, 13–14, 16, 24, 25, 122, 134–135, 142–143). As plaintiff's counsel suggested at the bar, this difference can be shown by analogy. Suppose a motion picture showed Mr. Justice Holmes on the bench deciding cases in a way that laymen would regard as eminently just and fair, but in a way that lawyers would say showed an unprofessional disregard of statutes, precedents, traditions and canons of judicial conduct. Would not Mr. Justice Holmes, were he alive, have a good cause of action for defamation? To be sure, all professional men have to stomach a certain amount of lay misrepresentation of their virtues. [Cf. Holmes-Pollock Letters: vol. I, p. 106, letter from Holmes to Pollock, Sep. 23, 1902; vol. I, p. 107, letter from Pollock to Holmes, Oct. 3, 1902.] Yet there comes a point when what the layman regards as a statement of virtuous conduct, a professional regards as portrayal of a vice—and not necessarily, from the professional approach, a venial vice. And the law recognizes that the professional man's interest in not having added to his career imaginary facts that tend to lessen his colleagues' opinion of him, rises superior to the motion picture producer's interest in embellishing a true story with colorful episodes not plainly stamped as imaginary but designed to increase the popularity of the motion picture.

Yet it is said by defendant's counsel that the motion picture will pass through even this needle's eye. He says that the profession would—and the Court therefore should—look at the picture as a whole; that it would regard the main theme as the account of a motorboat torpedo squadron as a unit in the Philippines; that it would not suppose that every single trait of Lt. **Kelly** (as he then was) was accurately pictured in the character of Ryan; and that even a professional officer would come away with a sense of what a hero and what a credit to the Navy Lt. **Kelly**, alias Ryan, was.

I concur that it would be unsound to isolate each single episode, action and utterance of Ryan and ask whether an audience of professional Navy men would say

Appendix 2

that that single item was unbecoming an officer and gentleman. But I do not agree that an audience of professionals would say They Were Expendable was purely a picture of corporate accomplishment by a squadron and that the individuals had more or less fictitious attributes. I am of the view that like the general public, the officer group would identify Lieutenants Bulkeley and **Kelly** with the characters Brickley and Ryan. And I think they would go away from that showing of the movie with a clear picture of the difference in professional standards of the two naval officers represented by the two principal characters on the screen. They would conclude that each had a brave heart but that Lt. Bulkeley was a self-controlled responsible officer, but his executive officer had a temperamental streak which occasionally carried him just out of bounds. I am not led to a contrary conclusion by defendant's argument that letters from high naval officers showed approval of the picture. The fact that the picture was liked by a certain number of naval officers seems to me irrelevant—they were considering the picture as a whole and its treatment of the service as an entity, not approving of the professional conduct of each character. Moreover, some of those naval officers were no doubt more mindful of the virtues of publicity for the Navy than of the rights of each separate individual to be fairly portrayed.

Indeed so far as I can tell, the difference in treatment of Lt. Bulkeley and plaintiff may be the real clue to why this action was brought. There were so many truthful elements in the picture of the two men that the average naval officer might suppose that the contrast in adherence to professional canons also tended to be true. Thus the representation was an example of the maxim, "the greater the truth, the greater the libel."

This explanation is indeed the only one that is consistent with the type of man Commander **Kelly** revealed himself to be not only on the PT boats in the Pacific but also in his attempts to avoid publicity by the Navy and in his behavior in the courtroom in Boston. Here he showed candor, modesty, courage, simplicity and presence of mind such as one rarely sees on the witness stand. Typical of Commander **Kelly's** composure under the stiff test of cross-examination by defendant's counsel, Mr. McClennen, is the following passage:

Mr. McClennen: "When you got back from the Philippines in the spring of 1942, you had been in some truly heroic exploits in the Philippines, had you not?"

Commander **Kelly**: "I presume that depends upon one's interpretation of heroic. It had been considered such by my superiors."

Mr. McClennen: "And you considered them such, didn't you?"

Commander **Kelly**: "I considered it line of duty" (R. 77). Or consider the dignity (apparent to everyone in the courtroom) with which Commander **Kelly** met Mr. McClennen's question on whether plaintiff recalled any act of his "indicating as much heroism, self-sacrifice and human concern at one time as is portrayed" in the motion picture. "I have never been accustomed to consider any of my acts as having been heroic" (R. 160).

11. But defendant says that even if the picture did hold plaintiff up to ridicule or otherwise defamed him, plaintiff gave defendant a license to show just that picture.

Plaintiff did, after repeated requests including one from the Secretary of the Navy, execute Ex. 4, the letter of December 21, 1942. I cannot find that as a matter of law he was coerced to execute the document. However, in view of the fact that it was drafted by others to serve the interests of others, and that plaintiff was a most reluctant signatory, I conclude that the instrument should be construed as favorably to plaintiff as possible. The opening sentences of the letter make it evident that what plaintiff was waiving was only his right to privacy in those states in which such a right was recognized. That is, he was giving a license which would prevent him from making the particular type of claim which Mr. Brandeis and Mr. Warren in their famous paper, The Right to Privacy, 4 Harv.L.Rev. 193, had proposed to have recognized and which was urged (unsuccessfully) before the New York Courts by a person who thought he was depicted in A Bell for Adano. Toscani v. Hersey, 271 App.Div. 445, 65 N.Y.S.2d 814. Plaintiff was not giving up any claim he might have on account of the common law of libel (such as is covered in Restatement, Torts, Bk. III, c. 24–27) not to mention the common law of intentional infliction of mental distress (such as is covered in the amendments proposed to Restatement, Torts, § 46). Thus plaintiff was not making a surrender, waiver or license adequate to excuse defendant from liability for the defamation alleged in the case at bar.

Moreover, in my view the provisions of the license limited defendant to depicting plaintiff or a character that corresponded to him. I find as a fact that in essential elements of professional fitness Rusty Ryan does not correspond to plaintiff. Therefore, one of the terms of the license was not met. I need not consider in detail whether defendant met other terms of the license (1) by securing approval of the United States Navy; (2) by not elaborating the romance beyond the portrayal of it in Mr. White's book; and (3) by portraying as accurately as possible historical events. It will be sufficient for me to say that I find a failure of defendant to meet the third and last of those terms.

12. There remains the final question as to what damages plaintiff may recover on account of the showing of the motion picture at the Boston theatres. There is no evidence that those showings lowered his reputation in the eyes of anyone who had the power to promote his naval career. And no actual injury to his career has been shown. Indeed, the award of decorations, the making permanent of his rank of Commander and the assignment (R. 84) to teach at Annapolis all suggest that plaintiff suffered no appreciable damage in his profession.

Appendix 2

He testified that he did suffer social embarrassment in gatherings in Boston where there were guests who had actually seen or probably seen the movie. It is elementary that in Massachusetts as in most other jurisdictions plaintiff's mental anguish or suffering is an element of damage recoverable in a libel suit. Finger v. Pollack, 188 Mass. 208, 74 N.E. 317; Restatement, Torts, § 623; Magruder, Mental Disturbance in Torts, 49 Harv. L.Rev. 1033, 1055, 1056. But it has been said that "the injury to feelings which the law of defamation recognizes is not the suffering from the making of the charge, but is the suffering which is caused by other people's conduct towards him in consequence of it." Wigmore Evidence, Rev.Ed., 1940, vol. I, § 209; p. 704. If that were the law, then Commander **Kelly** could not recover because he has not shown that his injured feelings were the result of the conduct of persons in his profession who alone are the audience which I have found might have a lower opinion of him. But Professor Wigmore's statement does not state the law of Massachusetts. Marble v. Chapin, 132 Mass. 225; Curley v. Curtis Pub. Co., D.C.Mass., 48 F.Supp. 27. The most dramatic proof is Marble's case. Chapin falsely told Mary Cummings that "Mr. Marble has had intercourse with you." Miss Cummings knew it was not so; could not have had her estimate of Mr. Marble lowered by the defamation; and never repeated the statement. Yet Mr. Marble was allowed to keep a verdict for his mental suffering. In short, in Massachusetts let there be a finding that defendant published a libel and it follows that the trier of fact can award plaintiff compensation for the injury to his feelings, dependent upon the trier's estimate of plaintiff's sensitivity. Curley v. Curtis Pub. Co., D.C.Mass., 48 F. Supp. 27.

And as the trier of fact I find that plaintiff while possessed of an exterior that is calm, cool and collected has an inner spirit of fineness and distinction. Such persons suffer more than readily appears to those who customarily measure by the gross proportions of the motion picture world.

There is only one factor which in any way suggests that plaintiff is not of the fiber that I have pictured; and not entitled to have his suffering measured on that basis. That was his admission that he had applied for and been granted the Purple Heart as a recognition of a wound which, while it may have been service-inflicted, was certainly not the result of unusual risks peculiar to war. Defendant's counsel hammered hard on this point, and I believe with some justification. But I am not persuaded that plaintiff lapsed more than momentarily from his customary attitude of depreciating all types of self-advertisement.

Doubt as to plaintiff's sensitivity cannot be premised on his willingness to bring this libel suit. To be sure, many men of dignity, particularly professional men, are accustomed to face with a stiff upper lip public minor misunderstanding of their work. But men of the finest grain may feel that when calumniators have circulated false and mischievous canards about their official accomplishments or private lives a libel suit is justifiable principally to secure judicial declarations of the truth rather than substantial monetary damages. [Compare Theodore Roosevelt v. Newett, reported in H. P. Pringle, Theodore Roosevelt. A Biography (1931), pp. 573, 574]. Moreover, a man of the highest character and sensitivity may on the advice of counsel come into court and ask a large recovery for libel on the ground among others that that is the best way to attract public attention as prominently to plaintiff's ultimate vindication as public attention was orginally attracted to defendant's misrepresentation.

Since the only elements of damage proved relate to (1) loss of reputation among naval officers who attended performances in two Boston theatres and to (2) mental disturbance, the recovery cannot be of large proportions. Commander **Kelly** may, however, take some justified pride in a judicial finding that despite quite as gruelling a cross-examination as any witness is apt to face in court he stands out as a man of exemplary physical and mental courage, of self-restraint and self-discipline, remarkably indifferent to self-advertisement but understandably disturbed by widespread depiction of him as deserting the ideals of his profession and adopting the patterns of culture favored by the movie-going public. At the request of the Secretary of the Navy, Commander **Kelly**, agreed to sacrifice for the nation's good his privacy, as he would have sacrificed his life. But he was never asked to and never agreed to sacrifice his reputation as a "chevalier sans peur et sans reproche."

On the first count, judgment for defendant without costs.

On the second and third counts, judgment for plaintiff for $3,000 with costs.

BIBLIOGRAPHY

Anderson, Lindsay. *About John Ford.* London: Butler & Tanner Ltd., 1981.
Eyman, Scott. *John Ford: The Complete Films.* Los Angeles: Taschen, 2004.
____. *Print the Legend.* New York: Simon & Schuster, 1999.
Ford, Dan. *Pappy: The Life of John Ford.* New York: Da Capo Press, 1979.
Gallagher, Tag. *John Ford: The Man and His Films.* Berkeley: University of California Press, 1986.
Katz, Ephraim. *The Film Encyclopedia.* New York: G.B. Putnam's Sons, 1979.
Levy, Bill. *John Ford: A Bio-Bibliography.* Westport, CT: Greenwood, 1998.
____. *Lest We Forget: The John Ford Stock Company.* Albany, Georgia: BearManor Media, 2013.
Maltin, Leonard. *Movie Encyclopedia.* New York: Penguin, 1994.
McBride, Joseph. *Searching for John Ford.* New York: St. Martin's Griffin, 2001.
Place, J. A. *The Non-Western Films of John Ford.* Secaucus, New Jersey: Citadel, 1979.
Roberts, Randy, and James A. Olson. *John Wayne: American.* New York: The Free Press, 1995.

INDEX

Numbers in ***bold italics*** indicate pages with photographs.

Alper, Murray 20, 50, ***136***, ***137***
Anderson, Lindsay 27, 36, 39, 169, 193
Armistead, Mark 23
Arrowsmith 164

Baby Face 160
Back to Bataan 24
Barrat, Robert 14, 20, 55, ***127***, ***129***, ***130***
Barthelmess, Richard 55, ***141***, ***143***, ***144***
Bataan 29
The Battle of Midway 27
The Bells of St. Mary's 40
Bergman, Ingrid 42
The Big House 158
The Big Trail 15, 23, 160
The Blue Angel (Der Blau Engel) 24
Bond, Ward 14, 19, 24–25, 30, 34–***38***, 48–49, 54, 56, ***65***, ***68***, ***71***, ***77***, ***78***, ***79***, ***98***, ***99***, ***106***, ***115***, ***116***, ***118***, ***124***, ***125***, ***126***, ***129***, ***130***, ***145***, 160, 163, 164, 166, 186
Brannigan 162
Bulkeley, Rear Admiral John D., USN 28–29, 31, 34, 153–155, 172–175, 185, 188
Burke, Dan 9, 16
Busman's Holiday 159

Calling Dr. Gillespie 162
Capra, Frank 16, 165
Captains Courageous 158
Carey, Harry Sr. 22, 24
Cimarron 22
The Courtship of Andy Hardy 162
The Cowboys 162
Crisp, Donald 27

Dallas (television series) 163
Darwell, Jane 27
December 7th 26
De Cordoba, Pedro 20, ***86***, ***87***, ***89***
The Desperate Hours (play) 159

Destry Rides Again 23
DiMaggio, Joe 42
Dirigible 165
The Divorcee 158
Dr. Bull 24
Dolphin Street 162
The Donna Reed Show (television series) 163
Donovan, General William 26, 39, 162
Drums Along the Mohawk 24

Earl of Chicago 159
Einstein, Albert 42
El Dorado 161
Everson, Karen 5, 7, 9, 13–14
Everson, William. K. 5, 10, 13–14
Eyman, Scott 3, 7, 9, 11, 12, 27, 169, 193

The Fighting Seabees 24
Flesh 24
Flying Tigers 24
Fonda, Henry 22, 24, 27
Ford, Dan 10, 35
Ford, John 9–14, 16, 18–20, 22–31, ***33***, 34, 36–***38***, 39, 40, 42, 46–55, ***65***, ***68***, ***72***, ***73***, ***75***, ***77***, ***80***, ***83***, ***86***, ***91***, ***95***, ***97***, ***103***, ***106***, ***105***, ***106***, ***116***, ***130***, ***135***, ***141***, ***143***, ***144***, ***149***, ***152***, 155, 159–165, 168, 169, 178, 193
Fort Apache 22, 161–162, 164
Four Sons 29, 162, 174
Franklin, Sidney 28
From Here to Eternity 163

Gallagher, Tag 10, 30–31, 168, 193
The Gallant Hours 159
Gentleman Jim 164
The Get-Away 162
Gone with the Wind 164
The Grapes of Wrath 23, 164
Green Dolphin Street 163

Index

Hangman's House 162
Hawks, Howard 16, 164
Haycox, Ernest 23, 60
Here Comes Mr. Jordan 159
Hitchcock, Alfred 16, 159
Holt, Jack 14, 19, 51–52, *95*, *96*, *101*, *103*, *106*, *115*, *122*, *129*, *130*, *132*, 165, 167, 168
How Green Was My Valley 23
How the West Was Won 161
The Hurricane 24

The Informer 23
The Iron Horse 22
It Happened One Night 164
It's a Wonderful Life 162–164

Jesse James 22–23
Judge Priest 24

Kelly, Commander Robert B. USN 7, 34, 155–156, 171, 173, 175, 177–179, 181, 183, 185–191
Kennedy, John F. 156
Key Biscayne, Florida 11, 16, 18, 32, *66*, *84*, *133*

Lady for a Day 164
Lady in the Lake 159
The Last Time I Saw Paris 163
Leave Her to Heaven 40
Levy, Bill 9, 193
The Life of Jimmy Dolan 160
The Long Voyage Home 161
The Lost Patrol 29
The Lost Weekend 40
Lynch, Bert 52, 54, *73*, *79*, *80*, *82*, *83*, *116*, *138*, *139*, *143*

MacArthur, General Douglas 14, 20, 29, 31–32, 34, 39, 55, 153–155, 173, 175, 180, 185
MacKenzie, Jack 26
MacKenzie, Jack, Jr. 26
The Maltese Falcon 164
The Man Who Shot Liberty Valance 13, 16, 22, 161, 162
Mannix, Eddie 28
Mantle, Mickey 42
March, Eve 41
Maris, Roger 42
Mary of Scotland 24
McGuinness, James Kevin 28
McLintock! 161
MGM Studios 13, 16, 19, 28, 29–32, 36–40, 42, 52, 54–55, *73*, *138*, *139*, 155, 157–159, 162, 168
Miami, Florida 11, 18, 32, *33*, 36, 42, 45, 46–48, 55, 56, *61*, *65*, *112*, *152*

Mildred Pierce 40
Mr. and Mrs. Smith 159
Mister Roberts 164
Mitchell, Cameron 20, 53, *67*, *68*, *78*, *113*, *145*
Montgomery, Robert 4, 11, 14, 18, 19, 30–37, *38*, 39, *41*, 47, 50, 51, 52, 55, 56, *65*, *68*, *70*, *71*, *77*, *80*, *89*, *90*, *101*, *103*, *105*, *106*, *108*, *109*, *116*, *118*, *119*, *129*, *130*, *132*, *133*, *135*, *137*, *141*, *143*, *144*, *145*, *147*, 157–160, 164, 167, 168, 178
Mother Machree 162
Mrs. Parkington 162
My Darling Clementine 12, 22, 24, 164–165

Nichols, Dudley 27
Night Must Fall 158
Notorious 40

O'Fearna, Edward *69*, *75*
Office of Strategic Services (OSS) 26, 30
The Oklahoma Kid 23

Paramount 15
Parrish, Robert 25, 27
Pence, Chester 17, *136*, 158
Pennick, Jack 14, 19, 20, 24–25, 31, 52–53, *68*, *77*, *80*, *97*, *103*, *106*, *129*, *149*
Pichel, Irving 27
The Picture of Dorian Gray 162
Pilgrimage 24
Pittsburgh 161
The Plainsman 22
Power, Tyrone 22
The Prisoner of Shark Island 24
Private Lives 158

The Quiet Man 164

Reap the Wild Wind 25, 161
Red River Valley 14, 37
Reed, Donna 14, 19, 30, 36, *38*, *94*, 162–163, 167–169
Ride the Pink Horse 159
Rio Bravo 164
Rio Grande 14, 22, 161–162
Rio Lobo 162

Sahara 29
St. Pierre, Louis *17*, 54, *98*, *99*
Salute 163
Sands of Iwo Jima 161
Scutti, Nick 4, 9, 10, 14, *17*, 18, 19, 20, 24, 25, 31, 42, 43, 45, 52, 53, *62*, *65*, *67*, *72*, *75*, *77*, *80*, *88*, *89*, *95*, *96*, *97*, *98*, *99*, *101*, *103*, *106*, *119*, *122*, *126*, *129*, *130*, *136*, *137*, *139*, *149*, *152*
The Searchers 12–13, 22, 161, 164

Index

See Here, Private Hargrove 162
Sergeant York 164
Seven Sinners 161
Sex Hygiene 26
She Wore a Yellow Ribbon 22, 161–162
The Shepherd of the Hills 161
The Shootist 162
Simpson, Russell 14, 20, 37, *135*
Spellbound 40
The Spoilers 161
Stagecoach 13, 22–23, 35, 160, 162, 165
Stamford, Connecticut 9, 42, 47, 53, 68
Stamford Historical Society 9, 16
Steamboat 'Round the Bend 24
Straight Shooting 22, 39
Sturges, Preston 16
Sub Chaser Training Center 18, 42, 45–46, 55
Submarine Flight 165
The Sun Shines Bright 13

They Were Expendable (book) 19, *20*, 28–29
They Were Expendable (movie) 15, 18, 19, 20, 22, 26–32, 34, 36–40, 42, 46–48, 50, 52–54, 56, *59, 60, 62, 66, 68, 70, 72, 80, 82, 84, 88, 90, 92, 94, 98, 106, 110, 116, 122, 130, 136, 140, 144, 150*, 153–156, 158–169, 171, 174, 176–178, 186, 188
Thompson, Marshall 19, *33, 60, 62, 115, 116*
3 Bad Men 22, 39, 154
3 Godfathers 22, 161–162, 164

Tobacco Road 24
Torpedo Squadron 26
The Treasure of the Sierra Madre 165
Trowbridge, Charles 20, ***103, 105***
True Grit 161

Union Pacific 23

Wagon Master 12, 22, 164
Warner Bros. 15
Wayne, John 9–12, 14, 18, 19, 20, 22–25, 30, *33*, 34–37, *38*, 40, *41*, 47, 49, 51, 54–56, *67, 68, 71, 75, 77, 83, 89, 94, 98, 99, 101, 103, 105, 106, 116, 118, 130, 132, 135, 136, 137, 143, 144, 145, 147*, 155, 159, 160–164, 167–169, 178, 193
We Sail at Midnight 26
Wead, Frank Wilbur "Spig" 19, 27–28, 30, 39, 177, 183–184
Weekend at the Waldorf 40
Wellman, William 16
What Price Glory 24
When Willie Comes Marching Home 24
White, William L. 19–20, 28–29, 168, 174, 178, 185
The Whole Town's Talking 24
Williams, Ted 42
The Wings of Eagles 27, 162, 164
Wonder Man 40
Wyler, William 9, 10, 16

Yamamoto, Amiral 26
Young Mr. Lincoln 24, 164

www.ingramcontent.com/pod-product-compliance
Ingram Content Group UK Ltd.
Pitfield, Milton Keynes, MK11 3LW, UK
UKHW050524150426
5217IPUK00026B/1781